John Lyons' The Making of a Perfect Horse

Raising and Feeding

The Perfect Horse

ISBN: 1-879-620-59-6

Belvoir Publications Inc.
Box 2626
75 Holly Hill Lane
Greenwich, CT 06836 USA

Kellon, Eleanor V.M.D.
Raising and Feeding the Perfect Horse
Kellon, Eleanor V.M.D.
and the editors of John Lyons' Perfect Horse

ISBN: 1-879-620-59-6
1. Horses - Training   2. Horsemanship   3. Horses

Manufactured in the United States of America

John Lyons' The Making of a Perfect Horse

Raising and Feeding

The Perfect Horse

with Eleanor Kellon V.M.D.
and the editors of John Lyons' Perfect Horse

Belvoir Publications, Inc.
Greenwich, CT

Contents

Preface

Every experienced horseman knows that, when making an investment in a horse, the purchase price is the smallest part of the financial equation. Beyond that are the costs of upkeep (housing, hoof care, vaccinations and veterinary care), training expenses and, last but not least, the costs of feeding our partner. In years past, many horse owners thought that throwing a little hay over the fence was good enough. But research in horse soundness and performance has taught us that feeding our horse for optimal health is more involved than that. The topic of equine nutrition can be as dry as old bran or as inviting as a warm mash with molasses and carrots. In this book, we've tried to present you with a delectable, easy-to-digest smorgasbord of the most important nutrition information in a way that you can put to practical use.

And, sooner or later, the romantic temptation of raising a horse of our own overtakes most of us, and we find ourselves planning for a foal. Suddenly, the person with 20 years' show experience feels like a total novice — as maybe well we all should — because the process of foaling and raising a foal is awe-inspiring. We depend on good information, easily accessible and in a sensible format.

As important as this information is, there is one ingredient we couldn't include in this book — it's the gut feeling about how your horse should be handled. But, don't worry. God has put that inside you already. After all, He loves both you and your perfect horse.

John Lyons

The Lord is my shepherd, I have everything I need. He lets me rest in green meadows, He leads me beside peaceful streams. He renews my strength. He guides me along right paths, bringing honor to His name.
Psalm 23:1-3

Section I

Feeding
The Perfect Horse

1

Feeding Myths

*Old-timers' tricks and old-wives' tales
can hurt your horse instead of help him.
You need to know the facts about feed.*

It shouldn't be too complicated: You give the horse quality hay and grain, and he eats it. Unfortunately, regarding what to feed and how much, there's a good deal of misinformation. We will look at a few of the common myths and misconceptions about feeding.

Myth #1 *Horses need at least a little bit of grain.*

The horse needs a certain amount of calories, protein, fat, vitamins and minerals to do well. But it does not matter if he gets them from hay, grain or good pasture.

The difficulty in feeding only hay is that the density of the calories (calories/pound) is much lower than with grain. Therefore, a horse doing moderate-to-heavy work on a regular basis may not be able to eat enough hay to fill his calorie needs, so that horse will need calorie-dense grain. Otherwise, hay alone is just fine, provided you make sure your hay contains the proper levels of vitamins and minerals or you supplement them as needed.

Myth #2 *A one-pound coffee can is a good thing for measuring out a pound of grain.*

This was true years ago when coffee cans actually contained a pound of coffee (they are only 11 to 13 ounces now!) and when you were measuring out plain oats, since oats and coffee have about the same weight-to-volume ratio. But corn is much more dense than oats, so the same measure will weigh twice as much. Your old coffee can would have contained one pound of oats or two pounds of corn. Sweet feeds, also heavier, would have weighed 1½ pounds per can. On the other hand, bran is fluffier and lighter than oats. Two coffee-can measures of bran provide the same weight as one can of oats.

As long as you know the actual weight of the feed in one scoop, you can use any container for scooping, including a coffee can. You should always know what weight of feed you are giving your horse.

Myth #3 *Bran is nothing but a fiber source.*

Bran is far more than simply a fiber source (see Chapter 9). Bran is classified by the NRC (National Research Council) as a high-energy feed for horses, and with good reason. Pound-per-pound, it provides more calories than average-grade oats, slightly less than corn and about the same as most sweet-feed mixes. Bran also contains excellent levels of many important minerals (magnesium, copper, zinc, selenium, manganese), although you will need to supply supplemental calcium to balance out the high phosphorus content.

The fiber content of bran is of a type that holds a lot of water, so it "bulks up" and softens the stool, stimulating the colon.

Myth #4 *Plain salt blocks give horses all the salt they need.*

While it is true that constant access to salt (and fresh water) is a must for all horses, voluntary salt intake, especially in extremely hot weather or if the horse is being worked, may not be adequate. On the other hand, it is potentially harmful to force salt intake by mixing it with the horse's grain.

While providing a salt block in the pasture or stall is a good idea, your horse may need additional salt, depending on his workload and the ration you are feeding him.

The horse should be regularly checked for signs of dehydration in hot weather. These include sticky/tacky-feeling gums and decreased skin elasticity. You can test skin elasticity with the "pinch test." Pick up a fold of skin along the horse's neck between two fingers. When you release it, it should quickly flatten back out. If it remains tented up or is slow to go back to smooth, flat skin, the horse may be dehydrated. If you suspect dehydration, get the advice of your veterinarian on safe ways to supplement salt and other electrolytes (see Chapter 13).

Myth #5 *Trace mineral (red) salt blocks provide all the extra minerals a horse needs.*

All horses must have access to supplemental salt, which is vital to equine health but almost non-existent in many common horse feeds, hays and grasses. However, mature horses at maintenance (not being worked) seldom need trace-mineral supplementation, unless the weather is exceptionally hot (causing heavy sweating). Young (growing), pregnant and actively exercised horses, on the other hand, often do need supplements, and you should consult your veterinarian to determine their correct mineral intake.

Many people mistakenly set out "red" livestock mineral/salt blocks. However, "livestock" blocks are not properly balanced for horses — they're too high in zinc, too high in iron (which is what makes them red) and too low in copper.

The best way to meet a horse's salt and mineral needs is to provide free-choice access to a plain white salt block, along with a balanced diet and plenty of fresh water. To ensure correct mineral intake, use a grain, complete feed or mineral-mix supplement specifically designed for your horse's mineral needs; also, be sure to select a product balanced for the type of hay you are feeding (alfalfa or grass). Heavily exercising horses, particularly in hot weather, may also need an electrolyte supplement specifically designed to replace the salt and minerals lost in sweat.

Myth #6 *Oats are the best type of grain to feed horses.*

Oats are a good choice, but there are certainly other grains that work as well. Corn is a good choice if the horse has difficulty holding his weight. Barley has slightly more energy and protein than oats.

Local prices for various grains may make one a better choice than the other. Whatever you choose, make sure it is of good quality and free of dust.

In order to know the right amount of feed for your horse, you'll have to be able to weigh the feed. As long as you know the weight of the feed you are giving your horse, the choice of scooper or coffee can is a matter of personal convenience.

Myth #7 *Feeding corn makes a horse hot.*

People mean different things by this. If by "hot" they are referring to body temperature (as in, "You can't feed corn in the summer; it's a hot feed"), there is some truth to that. The process of digesting corn does generate slightly more heat than oats, but it's not a significant amount. If you regularly use corn, and its price fits your budget better, go ahead and feed it.

But, if "hot" refers to temperament, the statement is at best a half-truth. Corn is much more energy-dense than oats (3.38 Mcal/kg of digestible energy compared to 2.85 to 2.99 for oats) and also weighs about twice as much. This means if you feed corn in the same volume as oats, you're feeding much more energy (calories). So, it isn't the corn, it's the amount of corn (or any feed) that may give the horse too much energy. The solution is to always substitute corn on a weight basis, not by volume.

Myth #8 *Feeding grain makes horses "tie up."*

Experts do not know enough to say with certainty what really makes horses subject to tying-up (a problem characterized by muscle spasms). We do know it seems to involve an overproduction of energy in relationship to the amount of work being done, or to the level of excitement. This runaway metabolism results in the over-contraction (spasm) and inability of muscles to relax.

Muscles use carbohydrates as their major fuel. They store it right in the muscle, in a form called glycogen. Glycogen is manufactured from glucose that is taken from the blood. Glucose is a simple form of carbohydrate.

Grains are easily digestible carbohydrates (easier, at least, than hays). However, the body also turns proteins and fats into glucose as needed for energy or building glycogen stores in the muscle. It is not at all clear if the form of carbohydrate the horse eats has anything to do with tying up (hay is 80% to 90% carbohydrate also, but in a less easily digestible form). However, you should always take care to cut grain or eliminate it on days a horse does not work.

Cutting grain drastically at other times only deprives the horse of the energy he needs to function and does not address the real cause of the tying-up problem. A better nutritional approach for horses that tie-up is to supplement vitamin E; selenium (get guidance first, as local soil levels vary in selenium level, and this mineral becomes toxic in quite low amounts); the B group of vitamins, especially thiamine; and critical minerals, such as potassium, calcium and magnesium.

Myth #9 *Horses should be fed twice a day.*

The common twice-daily feeding schedule is more for human convenience than for the benefit of the horse. The horse's system is made to eat virtually constantly. Left on their own, horses will spend about 80 percent of their waking time eating (or looking for something to eat). The horse's stomach and upper intestinal tract have a relatively small capacity, which makes it necessary for the horse to spread out his daily intake of food over the day. Many cases of colic (not to mention behavior and weight problems) might never occur if the horse is fed more frequently, keeping the total daily amount of hay and grain the same. If you can feed three times a day instead of two, do it. More frequently is better yet.

Myth #10 *All sweet feeds are about the same.*

Sweet feeds vary greatly in their nutritional value. Sweet feeds have been referred to as "floor sweepings and molasses," and sometimes this is not far from the truth. Some feed mills use inferior-grade grains when making sweet feeds, while other mills are rigorous in their formulations.

A sweet feed may also vary widely from batch to batch in the types of grain it includes. Protein content may be boosted by using either soybean meal or alfalfa meal, depending on availability and cost, resulting in different amino-acid compositions between batches.

While abuses exist, this is not to say you should not use sweet feeds. Horses love them, and the molasses itself has important nutritional benefits. However, you should buy a brand of sweet feed that comes with a detailed "guaranteed analysis" on the label. This usually means you will have to go with a large company rather than a small local mill.

Weighing grain

Here are three ways of knowing the weight of grain you are feeding:

1. *The easiest is to take a small plastic bag of grain to the feed or grocery store. Pour the grain onto the scale until it reads exactly one pound. Put that one pound of grain into a separate self-sealing plastic bag, and mark it as one pound. That becomes your standard for that particular feed. Do the same with each feed (oats, corn, bran, pellets, cubes, etc.) that you will be feeding.*

When you get home, transfer that one pound to whatever measure you will be using — a coffee can, milk container or plastic scoop. Then, with a permanent marker, mark that line on the measure. From then on, you'll know what one pound of that feed looks like in that container.

2. *An alternative is to purchase a scale to keep in the feed room. If you do this, it is most helpful to get a scale that can weigh more than small amounts, so you'll be able to weigh hay, as well as grain.*

3. *If you are feeding a number of horses or a variety of feeds, you may want a "Scale Scoop" (Agri-Pro Enterprises) instead of a scale for the feed room. As the name indicates, this is a combination of scooper and scale. It can weigh up to seven pounds of feed in one measure.*

It is easy to get the right amount of feed with a "Scale Scoop." You scoop down into the feed, then sprinkle out the excess until the gauge reads the number of pounds that you wish to feed. When the scoop is level, the reading is accurate. The "Scale Scoop" works equally well with grain, pellets or cubed feeds. ⊞

For contact information on specific products mentioned, please see page 204.

2

Secrets to Buying Good Hay

Hay is the heart of the horse's diet.
Without a quality roughage, you'll spend lots of
money on supplements
to make up the difference.

Although hays vary in their specific characteristics depending on the type, there are general rules you can use to determine the quality of hay. **Hay should be green. Yellowed hay indicates that the hay is aged and has lost valuable nutrients.**

Just how green it will be depends on the type of hay. In general, alfalfa is a deeper shade of green than grass hays. Alfalfa hay that has been treated with preservatives, such as propionic acid, is a bright, vibrant green (the propionic acid does not harm the horse or the hay).

The most nutritious and easiest-to-digest hays are those with a high proportion of leaf to stem. This is easiest to see in alfalfa where the leaves are small and appear in clusters that appear different from the stick-like stems. In grass hays, you will have to look a little more closely. The leaf/blade is thinner and flatter than the stems. Hays that have more stem than leaf are not as nutritious.

Stems themselves also help you determine the quality of the hay. **Very thick, long and tough stems come from plants that are old (at their full growth), while shorter, thinner and easier-to-bend stems come from young plants. Young plants are more nutritious.** The proportion and thickness of stems is most important when evaluating alfalfa, as alfalfa stems become more wood-like as the plant matures. With grasses, the larger stems are more digestible than those of alfalfa, as they often contain a reserve of nutrients for the plant.

Farmers pray for sun-
shine after cutting hay,
so it can properly cure
or dry before being baled.

The age of the plant when it was cut influences the quality of the hay as well, especially the protein content. Young plants that have not yet developed blooms (alfalfa) or seed heads (grasses) have a higher protein content. All of that affects how much hay we have to feed. Our chart at the end of this chapter illustrates what we mean.

You would have to feed a 1,200-pound horse in light work about 24 pounds of alfalfa or a 50/50 mixture of alfalfa and a good grass hay each day to maintain his condition, but 32 pounds of late-cutting (old plants) timothy hay to get the same result. As you can see from the list of supplements needed, older timothy hay has lost other nutrients besides calories.

Unwanted stuff

You should also check the inside of each hay bale. **Moldy hay often looks fine on the outside**. When you pick up a moldy bale, it will be heavy (rocks and dirt baled into the hay also increase the weight of a bale). Upon breaking it open, moldy hay will be difficult to split into individual flakes. The center may appear matted and discolored — often a grayish color. **Puffs of "dust" that come out of the hay when you pull the bale apart indicate either dirt or mold.**

It is especially important to check for evidence of rodent infestation. Mice like to make nests in hay. You may notice that a small area on the surface of the bale has been eaten away to make the entrance to the nest. Nests are usually located not too deeply in the bale, inside just a few inches. **Never buy hay that has evidence of rodent infestation and, if you should come across an individual bale with these signs after you get the hay home, either throw it away or take it back for credit.**

FOR HORSES IN LIGHT-TO-MODERATE WORK, OR "WEEKEND WARRIORS," GRASS HAYS SHOULD PREDOMINATE.

Dead mice are a source of botulism — the organism proliferates in their intestinal tract after they die and produces the botulism toxin. Removing the little carcass will not necessarily remove all traces of the potentially deadly toxin. Also discard or return any bale with any evidence whatsoever of animal parts (i.e., rabbits, mice) such as bones, fur, etc. for the same reason. A large outbreak of botulism in horses in California a few years ago was traced back to rabbits that had been killed by the harvesting equipment and inadvertently baled into the hay.

You should also avoid hays with a high percentage of plants that cannot be accurately identified, such as weeds, which often make hay less palatable. (Horses will not voluntarily consume weeds until the better-tasting grasses are gone from a pasture.) Weeds often also contain irritating substances such as thistles or burrs. The effect they have on the nutritional value of the hay is impossible to predict and depends on such things as precisely what the plants are and what stage of growth they had achieved when the hay was made.

Hays infested with insects should always be avoided. Of particular concern is blister beetle infestation. Depending upon the exact species of the blister beetle, even a small number can make a horse seriously — even fatally — ill.

Blister beetle warning

Blister beetles are a common parasite found on many plant and vegetable crops — from soybeans to watermelons. They are attracted to flowers, which is why they are usually found in third and fourth cutting stages of alfalfa.

The blister-beetle toxin (cantharidin) destroys the lining of the horse's kidneys and intestines if he eats enough. It actually takes toxin from about 30 to 50 male beetles (or over 250 to 1,000 of the less-toxic species) to kill a horse, although eating as few as three can cause severe colic. Blister beetles can also cause poisoning and even death to other farm animals, such as cows and sheep. However, it takes much larger amounts of the toxin to do this.

First- and second-cutting hays are the safest (assuming that the second cutting was made before the plants flowered). The bugs breed in July, making the cuttings from the end of summer most likely to be infested.

Blister-beetle larvae need grasshopper eggs to survive, and blister-beetle numbers will be the greatest the year following a heavy grasshopper infestation. Crimping and processing equipment can crush the beetles, releasing their poison, which then remains on the hay and is just as potent as when the bugs were alive.

Choosing a type of hay

Many properly cured hays are appropriate for horses. The ones we have listed in our chart at the end of this chapter are those for which the most nutrition information is available from the NRC. In general, alfalfa and alfalfa-mix hays are most suitable for breeding animals, pregnant mares, lactating mares, growing horses and high-performance horses.

For horses in light-to-moderate work, or "weekend warriors," grass hays should predominate. Grass hays also have the advantage of allowing you to feed more without the horse putting on too much weight.

Dollar value

The best buy is the hay that gives you the most for your dollar. However, this is not necessarily the hay with the lowest price per bale. If you have a choice between a high-quality mid-bloom alfalfa hay or a late-cutting grass hay that costs a dollar or so less per bale, the alfalfa should win, because you have to feed seven to eight pounds more per day of the grass hay to keep weight on the horse and more supplements will be needed for the poor-quality hay.

What "cutting" means

Hay is often described by the cutting. Hay fields can be cut and baled multiple times a year. The first cutting refers to the hay obtained the first time that field was cut and baled for the year; second cutting is the second time, and so forth.

*Many horsemen like to avoid first-cutting hay because weeds may be more numerous and also because the high moisture content can make it more difficult to properly cure, resulting in a higher likelihood of mold. While these reservations are generally true, you can still find first-cutting hay that is of excellent quality. **In fact, first-cutting hay is likely to be the most nutritious. Do not avoid first-cutting hay as a rule; just remember you must be especially careful to check for weeds and mold.***

Nutritional value

There is no single perfect hay. Alfalfa is rich in calories and energy but has a high calcium content that could lead to mineral imbalances and the need to supplement phosphorus and/or magnesium.

Alfalfa is also insufficient in the key trace mineral zinc, as well as selenium and vitamin E. High-quality grass hays can work well in terms of total protein content and energy, but the amount of lysine is unknown for many of them, so this essential amino acid should be supplemented, especially with young and working horses. Also, calcium levels are often borderline, and selenium, zinc, copper and vitamin E are often too low.

Mixing hays is often the most economical approach to take. If you feed 2 kg (4.4 pounds) of mid-bloom alfalfa hay (or 4.4 pounds of alfalfa cubes) and about 10 kg (22 pounds) of a high-quality grass hay, you will achieve a good calcium-phosphorus ratio, plus adequate amounts of major minerals, as well as copper and zinc levels that are close to NRC recommended levels.

For example, if your grass hay was a mid-bloom timothy, you would be fine for all the major and minor minerals — except for selenium in selenium-poor areas of the country — and would only have to supplement your horse with vitamin E and selenium.

Making up the difference

Unfortunately, many people have to take what they can get when it comes to hay, making up the difference with alfalfa cubes, pelleted hays or bagged hays. If these are unavailable or outside your budget, our chart at the end of this chapter will help you to determine what supplements you should feed.

A good supplement for mature horses doing no or light work and on a hay-only diet is Opt-E-Horse (Weaver Leather). This contains the key trace minerals zinc and copper, as well as vitamin E and selenium, and can be safely fed to horses on either alfalfa, grass or grass-and-alfalfa mixed hays.

For breeding or growing animals, or horses with a heavier work load, a broader-based supplement that addresses needs for other minerals as well as protein and key amino acids would be a better choice. Triple Crown 30 (Equine Specialty Feeds) is good for such horses on a grass hay or mixed grass-and-alfalfa-based diet. Select I or Select II (Select The Best) are two other supplements that are specifically designed to complement either alfalfa-based or grass hay-based diets.

Finding a good supply of hay

Hay can be obtained from various sources — auctions, tack/feed supply stores, by private purchase from a farmer or from a hay and straw broker. As much as is possible, **keep your horse's supply of hay relatively unchanging. Switching rapidly from one type of hay to another can cause digestive upsets such as bloating, diarrhea or even mild colic.**

Beyond that, the new hay will not be digested and utilized as well, meaning that you are wasting money. This is particularly true if you are changing from grass to alfalfa hay or from a poor-quality grass hay to a higher-quality one.

The most reliable way to keep your hay supply constant is to find a farmer in the area who is willing to sell you hay year-round from the same fields. If you can do this, it is worth the money to have the hay analyzed for its nutritional content

If they haven't been covered, round bales may be weather-damaged on the outside.

(protein, minerals, some vitamins) so that you know specifically what to supplement. You should at least try to locate a broker or store that purchases most of its hay from one or more constant sources or geographical areas. This will help keep the mineral content of the hay within a somewhat reliable range and make it worthwhile to have a hay sample analyzed once or twice a year to help determine supplement needs.

Another way to help keep your hay fairly constant is to buy it in large shipments. For people with only one or two horses this is not practical, but you may be able to locate other owners in your area who would be willing to split a large load. Buying hay in this way, directly from a farm or at auction, is also the most economical.

To avoid over-aging and loss of nutritional content of the hay, do not buy more than you can use up in a few months time.

Only buy hay that has been completely "cured," never a load that the seller tells you needs to "sweat" or be stored for a while before you can feed it. Statements such as this mean that the hay was baled with too high a moisture content. Odds are that if you buy and store it, when you get around to using it, a large percentage of the bales will have molded or "cooked" to a brown crisp. **Wet or molding hay is a severe fire hazard.**

Another precaution for buying hay at auction is to ask when the hay was baled. Many farmers, having sold or fed the best hay already, will take hay from the year before to auction to make room for the present year's crop. This is particularly a danger in the spring. All hay purchased in late winter/early spring will be from the year

Recommendations for a 550-kg (1,200-pound) horse at light work

TYPE OF HAY	AMOUNT TO FEED DAILY

50/50 Alfalfa and orchard grass   11 kg (24.2 pounds)
Comments: Need to supplement selenium, zinc and vitamin E, probably lysine.

Alfalfa — mid-bloom   10.8 kg (23.6 pounds)
Comments: Need to supplement selenium, zinc and vitamin E. Calcium:phosphorus ratio is in the danger zone at 6:1.

Orchard grass — early bloom   11.5 kg (25.3 pounds)
Comments: Need to supplement calcium, selenium, zinc, vitamin E and lysine.

Orchard grass — late bloom   13 kg (28.6 pounds)
Comments: Need to supplement lysine, calcium, selenium and vitamin E.

Timothy — mid-bloom   12.6 kg (27.72 pounds)
Comments: Need to supplement selenium, vitamin E and lysine.

Timothy — early bloom   12.2 kg (26.8 pounds)
Comments: Need to supplement selenium, copper, vitamin E and lysine.

Timothy — late bloom   14.1 kg (31.68 pounds)
Comments: Need to supplement phosphorus, copper, zinc, selenium, vitamin E and lysine.

Brome — mid-bloom   12 kg (26.4 pounds)
Comments: Need to supplement lysine, calcium, zinc, selenium and vitamin E.

Smaller, finer stems are more palatable and nutritious than larger, stiff stems

before and will inevitably have lost some of its nutritional value, but properly cured hays will still be OK to feed for about 12 months after baling. Consider only loads that appear to be of good color. Purchase a few bales separately so you can open them and examine them more closely before buying the entire load.

An unscrupulous practice you should be aware of is the trick of loading the outside of a load with good bales, but packing the middle and back of the load with bales of poor quality. If you cannot get access to bales in this location before unloading the truck (and you often cannot, especially with large loads), be sure to get the name, address and phone number of the person selling the hay, and inform them you will expect a refund for unusable bales. If they will not agree, don't buy their hay. **PH**

For contact information on specific products mentioned, please see page 204.

Notes

3

When Hay Is Scarce

Running out of hay — sometimes simply locating it — is a huge frustration.
However, there are healthy alternatives.

You've waited until the last minute (again!) to get hay. You pull into the local farm store in your van, kids complaining in the back seat that they're hungry and too crowded because they have to make room for a few bales of hay. The radio warns there's a storm coming. You are already frazzled when the store clerk informs you they have been out of hay for days, don't know when to expect any to come in and don't have any idea where you can get some. Now what?

If you are having a day like that, you'll probably go back outside and have your car not start! Seriously, though, hay shortages can and do occur, and more than one person has found themselves in the situation of having their regular supply of hay run dry.

Horses need roughage

To feel satisfied, a horse needs to consume a minimum amount of fiber or "roughage." **The term roughage generally refers to those items that are high in fiber and relatively low in digestible energy, as compared to concentrates (grains)**. This translates into at least half of the diet being hay. If you deprive the horse of the fiber, he will not have a full, satisfied feeling and will continue to be irritable and look for alternatives — like any piece of wood he can get his teeth close to.

27

More importantly, the bacteria and other organisms that live in the horse's intestinal tract — and are critical to normal digestion and absorption of the diet — require fiber. Without an appropriate level of fiber in the diet, the beneficial organisms start to die off, and dangerous strains can begin to grow unchecked, resulting in a very sick horse.

Buying time

If you have any available pasture at all, even if the quality is extremely poor because of the time of year, turn the horse out. This will at least distract him somewhat, and he will amuse himself by picking at things usually considered undesirable — like tree bark and dried-up grasses. (Wooden fencing will be extremely appealing, also, unless the problem gets solved quickly!)

An exception to this recommendation would be pastures containing wild, unidentified plants. There are many, many species of toxic plants all over the United States that usually cause no problem

The "other side of the fence" — and the temptation to gnaw on the fencing — may look especially attractive to the horse without adequate hay or grass.

simply because they don't taste good to a well-fed horse, and consequently he will not eat them. **A very hungry horse is less selective about his diet, however, and most plant poisonings occur under exactly those circumstances.** Therefore, unless your pasture has been carefully maintained and seeded with grass species appropriate for horses, risks may outweigh benefits.

Even the worn-out pasture trick won't work for long. If you have to wait more than 24 hours to get more hay, you are going to have to come up with a substitute. This is no small feat, given the horse's sensitive digestive tract.

Poor substitutes for hay

Given that horses need roughage, what are your options if hay costs are too high and/or the quality of hay too poor in your area? A surprising number of things have been tried, many with success, some with less than ideal results.

Human food — Processed foods, such as breakfast cereals, breads, popcorn or any other for-human-consumption product you can think of won't work. Human food products are all very, very low in indigestible fiber. Furthermore, the natural complex carbohydrate in the original grains has usually been modified by the processing to make it easy for the human intestine to break down. If a large load of this type of carbohydrate is dumped into the horse's intestinal tract, the number of starch-loving bacteria will explode, levels of acid in the intestine will skyrocket, other forms of organisms will die, and your horse will be very ill.

Silage and haylage — Silage and haylage, often fed to cattle, are inappropriate for horses. Silage is made by harvesting mature but still green corn plants, which are then chopped up and stored in a silo. **Horses readily eat silage, but, unfortunately, it is not considered to be a safe feed** for them because the conditions under which it is produced are highly favorable to the production of botulism toxin, and even tiny amounts can be fatal to horses.

Haylage is made in the same way as silage, but with freshly harvested hay. Unfortunately, the same restrictions apply to haylage as to silage.

Cotton-seed hulls and peanut hulls — Cotton-seed hulls are the outer shells of cotton, and peanut hulls are essentially the outer shells of peanuts. Cotton-seed hulls and peanut hulls are roughly equivalent to ground corn cobs in terms of their nutritional value. However, the digestible energy of peanut hulls is lower, and there is also a risk of toxicity from aflatoxin production by molds, making peanut hulls largely unsuitable for horses.

If you are considering feeding hulls, be sure the feed provider understands your intended purpose for the product so that appropriate handling and storage procedures can be followed.

Paper — Believe it or not, ground paper (computer paper, corrugated boxes, etc.) is easily digested by horses. In fact, paper has a digestible energy content equal to that of alfalfa meal! The nutritional value essentially stops there, however, and ground paper would need to be heavily supplemented if used as a roughage. Feeding of de-inked paper is still in the experimental stages. **Paper is not recommended** as an alternative roughage for horses.

Now that you have a list of things that won't work, what do you actually do about that horse out there who's threatening to rip the barn apart if he doesn't get something to eat?

When choosing hay, carefully inspect it for mold or weeds. If good hay is in short supply, you may have to consider an alternative.

Acceptable substitutes for hay

Peanut-plant hay — To make peanut-plant hay, the above-ground portion of the peanut plant is cured (dried), then baled. Although it is not widely used, it may be readily available in your location due to a growing interest in it.

Let them eat straw — Straw is the stem and leaf portion of grain plants (oat, barley, etc.), which is cut when dried (yellow) and then baled. Although it might not strike you as a good alternative, **straw actually contains almost as many calories as hay**. If you bed on it, there will be no digestive problems with feeding extra straw (the horse will eat it — he probably already is to some extent anyway). Even horses not accustomed to straw will tolerate it well, as it is not "rich" in such things as readily fermentable carbohydrate or protein, which are likely to cause digestive upset.

Straw is not a good long-term solution, however, as a typical "hay belly" (straw belly, in this case) is more than likely to develop, and straw does not measure up nutritionally to hay in terms of vitamin, mineral and protein content. It would be like trying to live on popcorn — feeling satisfied, but not being very well-nourished.

Corn plants and ground cobs — Ground corn plants can make an excellent substitute roughage. Ground corn cobs are extremely high in fiber and provide about 50 to 75 percent as much digestible energy as grass hays. Their nutritional value essentially ends there, however, as protein and major mineral levels are extremely low. When ground with the ears, the composition is very similar to average nutritional values of grass hays, and minimal supplementation is necessary. Leaving out the ears and husks decreases the nutritional value somewhat and requires more supplementation. In any case, contamination by moldy corn could severely limit the usefulness of this roughage, as **even minute amounts of the moldy-corn toxin can cause death in horses.**

Note: There are periodic outbreaks of moldy-corn toxicosis and equine deaths related to moldy-corn contamination of grain rations. Take the risk of moldy-corn toxicosis into consideration when using corn products, making sure the product was formulated for horses.

Beet pulp — Beet pulp is what remains of the sugar beet plant after processing for the sugar. It is usually sold as shredded beet pulp and it resembles tobacco. Horses find beet pulp very palatable, and most

A beet-pulp mash can make a satisfying fiber substitute for hay.

digest it easily. In fact, beet pulp is commonly used as the base feed for horses with digestive upsets and allergies of all types, as well as older horses and performance horses.

Beet pulp can be soaked in warm water to plump it up and make a satisfactory and filling volume. Put about two pounds of beet pulp in a bucket, and add enough warm water to cover it completely, with an extra inch of water to spare. Let it soak for about an hour, then feed it.

Rice bran and wheat bran — Technically speaking, brans qualify more as concentrates than roughages because of their high digestible energy. Protein and mineral levels are also excellent in brans — higher in many cases than for commonly fed grains. To most people, perhaps the most surprising fact about rice and wheat bran is that the amount of fiber they contain is actually only about one-third as much as most grass hays, less even than highly concentrated, high-energy complete feeds (which run about 12% fiber). Brans are relatively light in weight, so it takes considerably more volume to equal the energy level in grains. For example, you must feed twice as much wheat bran as oats to provide the same number of calories if you are measuring your feed by the quart (or coffee can).

Rice bran provides 1.48 times the energy/calories as timothy hay, with wheat bran providing 1.66 times as much. Rice bran also has 1.5 times as much protein as timothy, wheat bran 1.79 times as much, and both are rich sources of the essential amino acid lysine.

On the mineral front, brans are rich sources of magnesium, manganese, selenium and zinc — a definite plus. Copper is a little on the low side, especially after you adjust for feeding less to avoid excessive intake of calories. **The major drawback to feeding brans is their high level of phosphorus and low level of calcium, which requires calcium supplementation to correct.** As with beet pulp, vitamins A and D will also need to be supplemented, although a bonus of feeding brans is that they're high in vitamin E and are excellent natural sources of the B vitamin complex.

As a substitute for grass hay, rice or wheat bran is so packed with calories and protein that you will need to cut the amount fed by about 40 percent to avoid excessive weight gain. However, since brans are so light, 18 pounds of hay translates into 10.8 pounds of bran, which is the same as 21.8 quarts.

Making changes

When making a change from your regular hay to an alternative roughage, substitution MUST be made gradually — at a rate of about one pound per day until at the desired level (be sure to substitute by weight, not volume, to allow for different densities of products). Making substitutions too rapidly (especially bran) can result in digestive upsets ranging from decreased appetite to constipation or diarrhea, even obvious abdominal discomfort/colic. This is because processing

Convenient to carry home from the feed store, bagged hay cubes are also tasty to most horses.

of roughages is done by the bacteria and other organisms that inhabit the extensive large intestine of the horse. For efficient digestion, the organisms must be allowed time to adapt to the new diet.

This is especially important in old or young horses (who may not have a very varied and healthy population of organisms), as well as in horses with any tendency toward digestive problems. You can help the horse make the adjustment easier by providing him with one of the probiotic products. These are composed of bacterial cultures, yeast and/or bacterial fermentation byproducts or combinations of these. Essentially, their function is to encourage and support the growth of those strains of bacteria and other organisms that are beneficial in the intestinal tract.

The easiest solution

Constructing a nutritionally sound ration around alternative roughages is hard work. On the other hand, there is a potential for saving money and at the same time actually getting nutritional benefits from the excellent mineral levels in things like beet pulp and rice or wheat bran. The need to balance these rations with supplements, however, cuts into the profit margin and complicates feeding.

A solution we feel is workable is to begin with a high-quality alfalfa hay (if not available, consider buying alfalfa cubes). *The high energy and protein content of alfalfa means that you can feed less of it with the same results. The high vitamin A, D and E levels and the high calcium also give you some room to work with when substituting alternatives. Here's how it could work.*

Beginning with a 950-pound horse, a ration of five pounds alfalfa hay, five pounds beet pulp and five pounds wheat bran per day meets or exceeds the maintenance NRC requirements for protein, energy, fiber, major minerals and fat soluble vitamins. No supplements are needed.

To find the content of any given nutrient, simply add the values for all three together and divide by three. Calcium works out to 1.24 + 0.62 + 0.13 = 1.989/3 = .66 (% calcium), and phosphorus works out to 0.57% for a Ca:Ph ratio of 1.38:1. This ratio is not quite ideal, but the total amounts of calcium and phosphorus are more than sufficient, so these substitutes can be safely fed to an adult horse during periods of hay shortage. In fact, some senior-horse feeds now also have increased phosphorus and somewhat decreased Ca:Ph ratios, because recent studies show that older horses have trouble absorbing their phosphorus.

Our crude protein works out to 15.1%, which is above the minimum of 10 to 12% required for maintenance in adults, but it's well within safe levels and leaves room for the horse to munch on his straw to his heart's content. Checking this ration out for all the other important vitamins shows our substitute meets or exceeds the NRC requirements for each. In fact, this mixture is appropriate for growing horses and horses in work, as well as throughout pregnancy and lactation, with the only exceptions being from weaning through 18 months of age and for intense work, where some grain will be needed to boost the energy density of the diet a little bit.

Note: The above pertains to feeding of the alfalfa/beet pulp/wheat bran combination alone, no added grain. If substituting this combination for hay in a diet that will also contain grain, it will be necessary to recalculate the total intake of calcium and phosphorus, as well as the Ca:Ph ratio. Feeding grain will most likely require that a source of additional calcium be provided to maintain a workable calcium-to-phosphorus ratio. Addition of grain could also push the phosphorus content of the diet into the danger zone (must be less than one percent of the total ration) and necessitate further adjustments (i.e., more beet pulp and less bran).

Commercial alternatives

Hay cubes and bagged chopped hays are the best alternative. If you search diligently enough, you will probably be able to find a store within a reasonable distance that has some in stock. Bagged forage products definitely cost more than bales, but they are usually of fairly high quality and readily accepted by the horse. Try to match the bagged product to the type of hay you were already feeding. Switching from a grass hay to alfalfa all at once is likely to produce some digestive upset, such as bloating and increased gas production, even some loosening of the manure. As a rule, this does not require any treatment but does make the horse uncomfortable.

Montana Pride and Trade One/Triple Crown (Triple Crown's product is also

Chopped alfalfa or grass hay is available bagged and can be used as the main hay portion of the diet.

grown by Montana Pride) both offer bagged alfalfa or grass forage products. Other manufacturers include First Thunder Feeds, West Coast Feeds, Canadian Agra Bio-Cubes and Tri-Forage Farms Ltd. Contact them directly for leads on suppliers in your area. If you still have difficulty locating the product, call the company back and tell them your problem. They usually go the extra mile to try to help you.

Complete feeds

A complete feed is designed to be fed without additional hay. It may be in textured (recognizable grains and pellets), pelleted or extruded form (a sort of a fluffed-up version of a pellet, similar to a chunk

or kibble dog food, containing fewer calories per volume — i.e., can per can or scoop per scoop — than pellets). This may seem like the perfect solution, but there may be problems.

Complete feeds contain a wide variety of ingredients — different grains, different roughage sources and grain byproducts that your horse may never have eaten before. Because of this, you can not rapidly switch the horse from his customary diet over to a complete feed without inviting digestive upsets.

If you truly have no other options, go to a feed store where the selection will be best. Try to find an extruded form rather than a pellet (you can feed more and thus keep the horse busy longer, and more satisfied). Tell the feed-store representative your problem and what your horse's regular diet was. Ask him or her to try to match that as closely as possible. If the store representative is not sure exactly how to advise you regarding how much you can safely feed, call the company directly and stay on the phone until you talk to someone who is qualified to give that advice. If the phone number is not on the bag, get it from the feed store. All things considered, this is probably the least desirable solution to the problem of no hay, because of the risk of causing digestive upset. ■PH■

For contact information on specific products mentioned, please see page 204.

4

Help Your Horse
Gain Or Lose Weight

*Could counting calories be the way
to help your horse adjust his waistline?
Or do other factors play a major role?*

When people go on a weight-loss plan, they write down everything they eat throughout the day. Before changing your horse's diet to help him lose or gain weight, you should do the same, and make a list of everything he eats — including his bedding, if he's bedded on straw. Next, of course, you also need a fairly accurate estimate of his weight.

Weight tapes can be helpful, but because of variations in body shape, they are less accurate than scales. So, where do you find a scale? Feed mills have truck scales for weighing loads of grain, as do various trucking operations such as national furniture-moving companies. Weigh your trailer empty, then come back and weigh your trailer with the horse inside. Obviously, the difference in the weight is the weight of your horse. Now you have a starting point.

Let's say you determine that your horse weighs 1,200 pounds. You're feeding him oats and hay, and you've used a scale to weigh the feed — 25 pounds a day of grass hay and eight pounds of oats. The weight of your total feed — 33 pounds per day — works out to be 2.75% of his body weight (33/1,200 x 100 = 2.75%).

The NRC (National Research Council) estimates minimal requirements for preventing malnutrition in the horse as:

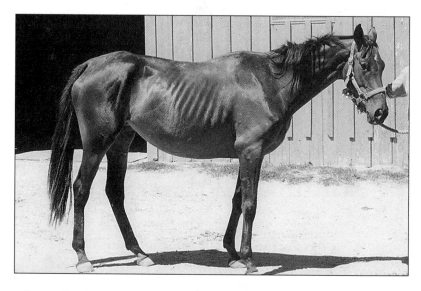

Obviously, this horse needs to gain weight, but loading him up all at once with feed would leave him in even worse physical condition. Weight gain should be undertaken in a systematic manner and ideally combined with moderate exercise.

- 1% of body weight per day for horses at maintenance (i.e., 10 pounds of food per day for a 1,000-pound horse at rest).
- 1.5% of body weight per day for average use (pleasure, show).
- 2% of body weight per day for heavy use (racing, endurance).

So, using our rough guideline, our 33 pounds of feed meet the needs for any work level. In fact, if we dropped the grain and fed only 25 pounds of hay, estimates show our horse can still support work (25 lbs feed/1,200 lb horse x 100 = 2.08%). But, as you will see, while some horses can maintain or even gain weight feeding at this level, for many horses, these numbers are too low.

Using the table on the next page, we can tell that our 1,200-pound horse at maintenance needs about 1.5% (18 pounds) of his body weight if feeding alfalfa or 1.8% (almost 22 pounds) of body weight if feeding timothy. If we feed two scoops/quarts of oats twice a day (each scoop just over a pound), our horse would only need 12.8 pounds of alfalfa to meet his maintenance needs. If we use the same volume (two scoops/quarts) of corn, he only needs about 4.5 pounds of alfalfa!

Now that we have saturated you with math and numbers, we will let up a bit and give you some basic guidelines for achieving weight gain or loss. But, it is important to realize there is a great difference in caloric content in common feeds, and which ones you choose and how you mix them can easily result in weight gain or loss.

Energy content of common feeds

Feed	Digestible Energy (mcal/kg)
Vegetable oil	8.98
Corn	3.38
Barley	3.26
Sorghum	3.21
Wheat bran	2.94
Oats	2.85 to 2.91
Rice bran	2.63
Beet pulp	2.33

Feed	Digestible Energy (mcal/kg)
Alfalfa hay*	2.07
Timothy hay*	1.77
Oat hulls	1.59
Straw, wheat	1.48
Straw, oat	1.47
Carrots	0.43

* average energy content of hays cut at midbloom

Feeding for weight gain

The principle is simple. To add weight to the horse, feed more calories than he uses. For most horses, this means adding a relatively concentrated source of calories, such as grain. On the flip side of this argument is the fact that horses are designed to eat grassy material, not grain, making it easier to accustom the horse to an increased hay intake than to an increased, or new, grain intake.

The easiest way to increase hay intake is simply to make sure the horse has hay available all the time. Compare what you were feeding to how much the horse will take in when given constant access to hay. For example, if you were feeding 20 pounds of hay a day and the horse was too thin, begin by increasing the horse to 25 or 30 pounds of hay a day. If this is gone before you feed again, the horse can probably eat even more hay. If you get up to over 30 pounds a day and the horse is still not gaining weight, he may not be able to eat much more hay. At that point, you will have to add a concentrated calorie source such as grain, bran or beet pulp to add the needed calories.

Concentrates (grains), however, must be introduced gradually to avoid digestive upsets. Begin with one to two pounds (NOT quarts or scoops, but pounds) once a day for a few days, then twice a day for a few days. Then increase by the same amount every few days, if needed.

Weight-gain aids

A popular, natural way to encourage weight gain in horses is to feed increased amounts of fat. Many weight-gain crystallized-fat products are actually animal fat. We suggest, instead, feeding vegetable fats to horses, but preferably not store-bought oils, as these have had their beneficial fatty acids destroyed by processing. A good choice is CocoSoya (Uckele Animal Health, Corp.), a blend of coconut and soybean oil that retains all the natural fatty acids. While any vegetable oil is usually palatable to most horses, this one is especially good for picky eaters, as it has a wonderful aroma that tempts them to eat. Start oils at 2 to 3 ounces a day, going up to approximately one cup, once or twice a day, maximum.

Probiotics, microbials and yeast are particularly valuable for horses with histories of digestive problems, such as recurrent mild colic or a tendency to appear bloated or pot-bellied.

Our favorite in this category is Ration Plus (S.E. Monroe, Inc.). It contains no actual live organisms, but is a fluid obtained from the culture of many different beneficial organisms, which encourages their growth in the horse's intestine.

Feeding for weight loss

Just as with humans, losing weight is often more difficult for horses than putting it on. To adapt your horse's diet for weight loss, the starting point is the same as for weight gain — calculate exactly how much the horse needs to maintain the desired weight at his age and level of activity. If you are feeding too much, cut him back to the appropriate amount for 1,200 pounds. If you are already feeding the appropriate amount for 1,200 pounds (or less), you will have to cut calories further.

Most weight-loss diets recommend that you eliminate grain and other concentrates entirely, feeding the horse only the amount of hay he would need to hold the correct weight. However, this leads to worsening of trace-mineral deficiencies (already common on hay-only diets), so you will probably have to supplement one or more of the minerals zinc, copper, manganese and selenium. **Horses on severely restricted diets may also need calcium, phosphorus and magnesium supplements, and all will need additional vitamin E.**

Decrease frustration at feeding time by providing your chubby pal with plenty of carrots when other horses get grain. Using shavings for bedding, instead of straw, is also a good idea. Many, if not most, horses on restricted-hay diets will resort to eating their straw, and while its vitamin and mineral content is dismal, straw has lots of calories — only 16 percent fewer than timothy hay!

Crash diets dangerous in ponies

The stereotype of the fat little pony is more often true than not. Ponies can survive on what would most definitely be starvation rations for most horses, and this makes their weight difficult to manage. The same is true of horses with pony-type metabolisms, such as Fjords, Icelandics, Morgans and so forth. However, extreme dieting with sudden and large cuts in energy intake can cause severe metabolic problems and even death in these animals.

Cut total caloric intake gradually, by no more than 10 to 20 percent at a time, and allow the pony to stay at that level of intake for at least a week before considering any further cuts.

Role of exercise

Weight loss in any horse is made much easier and faster when the horse exercises regularly. This is especially true for horses who have difficulty losing weight.

Turning the horse out in a field or paddock all day is not likely to meet his need for exercise. Twenty to 30 minutes a day at the trot, preferably daily, but a minimum of four days a week, will be needed to "reset" the horse's metabolism. A note of caution is in order with horses who are severely out of shape. Begin any exercise program gradually to avoid muscle pain or injury.

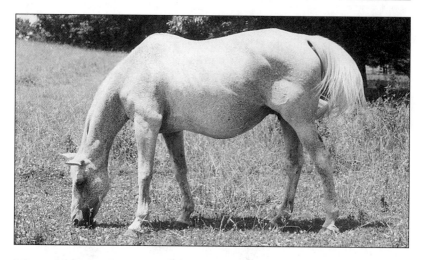

Mares in foal are not candidates for weight loss in most cases, nor are horses who have a "hay belly" but no excess weight along their topline. Even fat broodmares will lose weight dramatically as their foals begin to nurse.

Diseases affecting weight gain or loss

Every horse's teeth should be routinely checked, but especially so for any horse with trouble gaining weight. Also, aggressive deworming should also be instituted, as there are horses whose immunity to intestinal parasites is not up to par, even with a normally adequate deworming schedule.

Horses with long-standing, gradual weight loss may suffer from undiagnosed chronic disease. Lymphosarcoma (a form of cancer) or malabsorption (inability of the intestine to properly break down and/or absorb some foods) are rare, but should be considered if dietary changes and exercise don't work.

Excessive weight gain may be seen in older animals with pituitary tumors, although in this case the apparent weight gain is usually fluid accumulation, not fat or muscle. Thyroid problems do occur in horses, but don't give your horse thyroid supplements for weight loss unless recommended by your veterinarian. He may well lose weight, but only because he has become poisoned by the extra hormone. ◧

For contact information on specific products mentioned, please see page 204.

5

Tummy Troubles
On The Trail

*Whether all day on the trail or attending a show,
horses can be predisposed to colic
if owners forget the basics of feed and water.*

Horses are designed to eat almost constantly, spending up
to 80 percent of their waking hours just munching away.
The equine intestinal tract works most efficiently with a
steady flow of moderate amounts of feed — not long periods of fasting followed by a large meal, which is the typical scenario of a day-long trail ride or horse show.

When a relatively steady supply of forage is not available, and especially when an empty period is followed by a big meal, digestion
suffers. The horse may get anything from an uncomfortable feeling
to a serious intestinal disruption, leading to improper gut movement, gas build-up, the death of beneficial digestive micro-organisms and, of course, pain.

Obviously, not every horse gets to devote 80 percent of each day
to eating. Fortunately, as a reserve, the intestines maintain a large
volume of fluid and partially digested roughage. Also in this soup
are a wide variety of bacteria, protozoa and yeast, as well as electrolytes. The amounts of fluid and electrolytes fluctuate, depending on the body's needs during various activities. If the horse
stopped eating, it would take at least two days to empty his intestinal tract completely.

**The trick to avoiding colic when using the horse for long peri-
ods of time, such as on long trail rides, is to meet his minimum
needs by using the proper feeds and by recognizing that his body
has other needs as well.**

43

H₂O — life's liquid gold

Water is the single most important nutrient. **At rest, the horse needs eight to 10 gallons per day to keep enough liquid in his digestive tract to move things along properly and maintain the intestinal soup.** If he works for six to eight hours, even at low speeds, the water requirement for that day at least doubles. Factor in losses that occur from sweating and increased respiration (some water vapor is lost with each breath), and the amount needed can easily triple.

When you start out on a multi-day ride with a horse whose body has a normal level of water, his intestines act like a canteen, reserving water to use if his body water levels start to drop, which can happen after an hour or so of continuous work. The kidneys slow the production of urine, and water is absorbed from the intestinal tract, which helps keep the horse going comfortably between stops.

However, this system isn't risk-free. As water is "borrowed" from the intestines, their contents become more concentrated and bulky. Consequently, movement along the intestinal tract slows. If the intestinal "canteen" gets too low, colic can result. The horse must be able to refill his water reserves frequently.

Never set out on a long ride without knowing exactly where you can stop to water your horse, and we mean more than a quick gulp. He should be allowed to rest long enough for his first satisfying drink and then offered water every few minutes (or have constant access to water) for at least 15 to 20 minutes.

This will allow enough time for his stomach to fill, then empty, as the water is absorbed and distributed throughout the body. His body will then tell him if he needs to drink more. Allowing the horse to have a small amount of hay (a pound or so) will also stimulate him to drink more.

If you can take advantage of natural water supplies (streams), by all means let the horse take a drink. However, it is best to dismount either before or after crossing the stream and then allow the horse to drink. Horses permitted to drink with riders on their backs may become unruly and insistent around a water supply.

How much water

A horse working all day long, even if not at excessive speed, can need 20 to 30 gallons of water, maybe more depending on his size, his diet, weather conditions and how well-hydrated he was before the ride started. Do not ration his water. This is one time where you can trust the horse to know what to do. Let him have as much as he wants, with water available at all times when you're not working him.

There is still considerable debate about whether "water founder" is a real thing or not. Water founder supposedly occurs when a horse has been worked hard, is very thirsty and is allowed to drink all that he wants at one time, and is later found to have foundered. The truth is that the founder was probably caused by excessive pounding, but experts simply aren't sure what role the water might play.

A safe course is that if you have a horse who is excessively hot and thirsty, allow him about two to three gallons on the first drink, then walk him five to 10 minutes before letting him have a couple more gallons. Continue regularly offering him water until he no longer wants to drink. It is then safe to leave the bucket with him.

Electrolytes

The horse's intestinal canteen maintains more than a supply of water. It also holds electrolytes, which the working horse pulls from the intestinal fluid as his body needs them. However, just as with water, the supply of electrolytes is limited, and when the horse taps into it, the environment inside the intestines is altered. The body considers this to be the lesser of two evils when faced with the demands of working muscles, but if it is allowed to go on too long without restoring the intestines to their normal state, colic can result.

The intestines also have muscles along their length — muscles that need electrolytes just like the skeletal muscles do. Electrolyte imbalances can be just as devastating to these muscles, and this is yet another mechanism that can contribute to colic on the trail.

The horse cannot store electrolytes. The major need is for sodium and chloride — salt. Unfortunately, natural food sources cannot meet this need, which is why horses must have a salt block or loose salt available at all times.

Endurance riders give their horses electrolyte mixtures at rest stops to prevent exertion-induced imbalances. Most horses used for

Take advantage of watering spots along the trail and encourage your horse to drink.

trail/pack riding don't exercise as hard as the competitive endurance horse, so their electrolyte needs are easily met if they are rested, fed properly and given supplemental salt.

While away from home, offer your horse a mixture of 75 percent plain table salt and 25 percent "Lite" salt (a potassium source) along with his feed at least twice a day. Carry several pounds along and offer it in a separate container, like a pie plate or large bowl. The Lite salt serves as a bit of insurance for the horse who may not feel like eating as much hay as he needs.

The eats

When you are considering what to pack, it might be tempting to only bring grain and let your horse pick at whatever grass he can find as a substitute for hay. However, that would be a mistake, because he'd have to graze for at least 12 hours each day to get enough minerals, electrolytes, roughage and calories, which would not leave much time for sleeping and riding.

Just to meet his calorie needs, a horse working at a sensible pace (mostly walking, some slow trotting) on the trail for long days will need at least two percent of his body weight in hay. This would be 20 pounds for a 1,000-pound horse — a third to a half a bale.

Hauling hay around with you, especially in large amounts, is not practical in many cases. You will have to get a little creative.

Forgetting about the horse's calorie needs for the moment, he'll need a minimum of one percent of his body weight in hay per day to provide sufficient roughage and bulk just for normal digestion. If you know your horse will have about six hours per day to graze on good, naturally available vegetation, he will meet about half of his minimum requirement that way.

Using our hypothetical 1,000-pound horse with a 10-pound minimum hay requirement, we now need to provide an additional five pounds or so of hay to keep his intestinal tract healthy. The easiest way to do this is with hay cubes. That bulky half bale of hay was out of the question, but we can certainly manage to pack along enough hay cubes to give the horse five pounds a day.

The easiest hay cubes to find are alfalfa. If the horse is accustomed to alfalfa in his regular diet, and if he gets that full six (or more) hours of grazing on the trip, this would give him a roughage intake that is 50 percent alfalfa or less, which is fine. However, if he's not accustomed to alfalfa, provide him with the same type of roughage source that he gets at home. **Changing types of hay under trail conditions is inviting intestinal upset, if not obvious colic.**

So far, six hours of grazing and five pounds of hay cubes provide the minimum roughage required to keep your horse's intestinal tract functioning smoothly, but you've still met only about half of his

Sodium needs

Daily NRC guidelines for 1,100-pound horse

Activity	g Sodium	g Salt	oz. Salt
Maintenance, low heat	7.5*	22*	1*
Maintenance, high heat	15.0 to 22.5	44 to 66	2 to 3
Moderate work, low heat	15	44	2
Moderate work, high heat	22.5	66	3
Heavy work, low heat	22.5	66	3
Heavy work, high heat	30 or more	88 or more	4 or more

Some researchers think horses need twice this amount for normal health, which would be 15.0 g of sodium, 44 g of NaCl, or 2 oz of pure salt per day.

calorie requirements. Feeding grain can make up the difference, but you absolutely must avoid any big changes in how much grain you feed him, compared to what he normally gets at home.

To meet his minimal estimated calorie needs, the horse will require six to seven pounds of sweet grain mix (a little more, if you're feeding plain oats) in addition to his grazing and hay cubes. In fact, he could probably use more, but a slight weight loss is preferable to making a big change in his diet under trail conditions. Assuming it's a short trip, better to let him regain any lost weight when he gets home. If the horse is not used to getting this much grain, increase his usual ration by no more than two pounds, and make up the difference in hay cubes.

You can make best use of grain, and still keep it at a safe amount, by selecting the correct type of feed. A horse who gets no grain at home should get no more than two pounds of grain per day, in divided feedings, during the trip. The calories from the missing four to five pounds of grain can be made up with hay cubes. Assuming that about 1¼ to 1½ times as much hay cubes gives the same calories as grain, then four pounds of grain is equivalent to five to six pounds of hay cubes. Yes, that means a little extra weight and a little extra bulk to carry along; but if it makes the difference between having a colic problem and not having one, it is definitely worth the inconvenience.

It may be helpful to divide and pack up the horse's grain and hay-cube rations into daily containers. You can then dig into them and give the horse a little at each rest and water stop. This helps keep the horse satisfied and also is the best way to keep his intestinal tract functioning smoothly by avoiding large meals at the start and end of each day.

With an understanding of your horse's needs, good menu-planning ahead of time and a little creativity in the feeding schedule, it is possible to keep your horse comfortable, satisfied and colic-free on the trail or at a day-long horse show. **PH**

6

The Power Of Protein

There are more myths, misinformation and missing information regarding protein in the horse's diet than just about any other major dietary component. We'll sort myth from fact and show you how important protein is.

If you could drain all the water out of a horse's body, about 50 percent of what is left would be protein. Protein is found in every cell. Muscle is almost entirely protein. The brain is all protein, and so is DNA. The framework upon which minerals are deposited to build bone, tendons, ligaments and joint cartilage is protein. Even the hoof is an astounding 93 percent protein.

There is no question that adequate, quality protein intake is of vital importance to the horse. And none of these essential protein-rich body components can be built, maintained and repaired without adequate protein sources in the horse's diet.

Now, if protein is so great, how did all the "bad press" get started? Part of the reason is a message sent from nutritionists that horses don't require much protein in their diets. Fortunately, that view is gradually but steadily changing. The original belief was never based on sophisticated studies of how protein is used in the body and how much is actually needed, but on evaluations of typical diets of average horses who survive without any serious, life-threatening problems. Nutritionists concluded that those diets must be adequate.

"Adequate" is the key word here — adequate to sustain life and adequate to grow a foal into what, at least externally, appears to be a normal horse, but those diets are not necessarily optimal for the health and development of an athlete.

Another group with an interest in keeping protein intake to a minimum is feed manufacturers. The fact is that protein, especially high-quality protein, is the most expensive ingredient in any animal feed. Livestock feed manufacturers are geared toward keeping the cost of raising and maintaining an animal as low as possible, to keep production costs low. For a pig or beef cattle operation, cutting cost of feed by a few pennies a day can add up to a big difference in the bottom line when that animal is sold.

Extensive research with livestock other than horses documents not only how much protein is needed, but what specific kinds of protein encourage maximal, healthy growth and strong immunity. This research is heavily funded by organizations that want to keep costs down, to get the most out of their feed dollar — and who can blame them?

The problem is that raising and keeping horses is generally not an activity that falls into the high-profit profile. As

Insufficient amounts of the right kind of protein can lead to bone and joint problems, particularly as the horse ages.

a result, funding for basic nutritional research in horses is difficult to come by. It is clear that we need to know a lot more than we do about protein in horses. To begin with, what real data is available tells us that protein is not "bad" for horses.

Amino acids

The protein percentage on a feed-bag label really only tells you how much nitrogen is inside the bag. The nitrogen content of protein is what distinguishes it from other energy sources (carbohydrates or fats). If we assume that a 10% protein diet is adequate for a horse, does it mean that anything with 10% protein in it will do? Definitely not.

There are two basic kinds of protein — vegetable protein and animal protein. Let's say you have a certain weight of grain and a certain amount of fish, meat or dairy product that contain X grams of protein. The total weight of protein in each may be equal, but the proteins themselves are different.

Protein is built of many small units, called amino acids. The protein in your horse's coat is different from that in his muscles because of the different proportions of amino acids it contains.

Amino acids are classified into two basic groups, essential and nonessential. As you may guess, **essential amino acids are those that must be provided in the feed in a specific amount each day to replace those lost or used up. They cannot be manufactured by the horse's body.**

Nonessential amino acids are those that the horse can make himself, usually by enzyme reactions that change one type of amino acid into another by altering its chemistry, adding things here and there to end up with the amino acid that the body needs for a given purpose.

A GRASS-HAY-BASED DIET AND A 10%

PROTEIN GRAIN MIX DOES NOT MEET

THE MINIMUM PROTEIN RECOMMENDATIONS

SET FORTH BY THE NRC FOR HORSES

AT MAINTENANCE.

Why is this important?

A tiny change in the level of a single amino acid (such as from 0.2 percent of the total diet to 0.3 percent of the total diet) can have profound effects on growth rate and how well different proteins in the diet are utilized. Amino acids that carry this powerful degree of influence are invariably in the essential amino-acid group.

Ten essential amino acids have been identified for pigs, 17 for chickens, five for geese and 18 for people. We have confirmation of only one in the horse, although others are suspected. While no nutritionist will seriously argue that only one amino acid is essential in equine diets, we only have hard information about the amino acid lysine.

In addition to knowing the identity of these essential amino acids, food-animal producers also follow detailed guidelines about exactly how much of each is needed at every stage of growth. Formulas are often changed as often as every few weeks to provide the animal with the best amino-acid blend for that stage of growth. All we know in horses is that falling below 0.3% of the total diet for content of lysine results in poor growth in foals.

The correct total amount of protein and the correct amino-acid profile are important for more than growth in size and weight. **Without correct protein, bones and joints will not form normally.** The list of problems that inadequate protein intake can cause is as long as the list of body parts and systems that contain protein.

Protein is especially important for working horses. During exercise, muscle tissue is damaged to some extent, requiring protein for repair. The muscles also use certain amino acids as important energy sources during exercise. The amino acid glutamine is the backbone of the major intracellular (inside the cell) antioxidant-defense system and is used up in high amounts during exercise.

Protein is also needed to repair and build strong tendons, ligaments, joints and bones. Estimates of protein requirements in human athletes are anywhere from two to three times the requirements for more sedentary individuals.

What to do about it

We have bombarded you enough with the holes in available information about a horse's protein needs. It's time to come up with something reasonable to do about it. Obviously, we can't go out and do the research needed to fill in the gaps. We also can't just throw away current feeding practices and pull something out of the sky. What we can do is to take a look at the NRC guidelines as a starting point to make sure our horses are getting the minimum total protein amount they need, to make certain that lysine amino-acid levels are at least at the minimum, and to identify those horses who may have special protein needs.

The NRC recommends a maintenance protein level of 10 percent. This is roughly the protein level of plain oats and most commercially formulated feeds designed for horses at maintenance.

Common protein myths

∎ *Horses don't need protein. The horse may not require as much protein as a carnivore, such as a dog, cat, lion or tiger, but he does have an absolute requirement for adequate protein and the correct balance of amino acids. Your horse's hooves and coat are almost entirely composed of protein. Every cell in the horse's body contains proteins that have important functions. Even DNA, the genetic controller of every cell, is protein and requires protein to duplicate itself.*

Young, growing horses need plenty of protein.

∎ *The amount of protein in the diet depends on the type of grain you feed. Most people focus on the protein percentage in their grains and tell you the horse is on a 10%, 12% or whatever-protein diet. However, grains are usually less than half of the horse's daily food intake. Young pastures and high-quality alfalfa can easily contain 20% to 30% protein. Even if your horse is eating as much grain as he is hay, you must also figure in the protein contribution from the hay as half of the total. If you feed 10% protein grain but high-quality alfalfa and good pasture, a horse getting half of his total calories from that source and half from 10% protein grain will actually be getting a 15% to 20% protein diet!*

∎ *Excess protein causes bone and joint problems in growing horses. Totally false. In fact, it is a lack of protein and/or feeding low-quality protein with insufficient amounts of key amino acids that is likely to contribute to the development of bone and joint problems. This myth probably has its roots in the problem of people overfeeding concentrates to "force" early rapid growth, which is the real culprit, not the protein in those grains.*

> ■ *High-protein diets damage the horse's kidneys.*
> *This is a perpetual — yet still false — belief. It is true that the waste products of protein metabolism are handled by the horse's kidneys. However, if the horse's kidneys are healthy to begin with, they are more than capable of handling this — it is their normal job! Kidney disease of any type is rare in horses.*

Protein in feeds

If you are feeding alfalfa hay, with a maintenance feed or oats, your horse is actually getting more protein than the minimum, since alfalfa commonly runs at least 14% protein and probably accounts for most of the energy the horse is taking in. Alfalfa also has an excellent lysine content of about 0.8% (0.3% needed).

The lysine content of oats runs about the required 0.3% (corn is lower at 0.25%), and many manufacturers now guarantee that their grain mixes (sweet feeds) contain the required 0.3% of lysine, adding it if need be. (If the lysine content is known, it will be on the label. If it is not on the label, you can be pretty sure there is not enough lysine in the grain mix.) Therefore, our alfalfa-based maintenance diet is probably adequate, based on what we know so far.

If your horse needs a protein boost, but does not tolerate soy well, try a supplement based on milk, egg or whey.

If you are feeding a grass hay and a 10% protein grain, the picture is different. **The total protein percentage in a grass hay is often below 10 percent, and the later the hay was cut, the lower the protein will be.** Figures on lysine content are not available for many grass hays, even in the most recent NRC publication. Where figures are available, such as for Bermuda grass, they show this hay is too low (less than 0.3%). It is a safe assumption that a grass-hay-based diet and a 10 percent protein grain mix does not meet even the minimum protein recommendations set forth by the NRC for horses at maintenance.

With adequate pasture, the horse will get his minimum protein (young, rapidly growing pastures can be as high as 20% to 30%

protein). **In fact, the high-quality pasture protein is probably largely responsible for putting the "spring bloom" on horses who are turned out on high-quality grass.** However, as pastures decline, and certainly over the winter, a deficiency can develop. This is why more and more equine supplements are showing up with lysine on their labels. Everything from specific formulas for hoof health to general vitamin-and-mineral supplements now often contain lysine.

THE PROTEIN PERCENTAGE ON A FEED-BAG LABEL REALLY ONLY TELLS YOU HOW MUCH NITROGEN IS INSIDE THE BAG. THE NITROGEN CONTENT OF PROTEIN IS WHAT DISTINGUISHES IT FROM OTHER ENERGY SOURCES (CARBOHYDRATES OR FATS).

Practical application

If so many horses are actually deficient, at least under some circumstances and for portions of the year, why don't they have more problems related to this? Maybe they do.

We already mentioned that the hoof is 93% protein. Lysine and the sulfur-containing amino acids such as methionine are critical to formation of healthy hooves. Do you know any horses with hoof problems?

Adequate protein is also essential for healthy skin and coat. Does your horse have as much shine and bloom as you would like?

On a more specific front, does your horse's urine ever have a really strong ammonia smell, especially in the deeper layers of bedding? **Excessive ammonia production is a sign that protein is not being utilized correctly; that some is being lost instead of used.** This is a classic symptom of amino-acid imbalance in the diet, and lysine is closely tied to the correct processing of other amino acids.

Many other nutrients can influence problems such as these. For that matter, excessive ammonia production can be caused by too much protein intake as well as improper amino-acid balance. However, if your horse's diet is otherwise adequate and you have problems such as these, suspect inadequate protein first.

We cannot go into details of all the different situations that could call for increasing your horse's protein intake. We would only be speculating. We can, however, discuss protein needs and exercise. The NRC has changed how it looks at protein and the exercising horse. **Recommendations are that the horse in work may need 12%, or even as high as 16%, protein to meet the increased demands of exercise.**

Nutritionists are divided on this point, some seeing the value of protein and others claiming it is not needed. They will likely continue this argument indefinitely, simply because the research to prove or disprove either opinion has not been done. However, facts known from other species and plain common sense would seem to indicate that a horse who is vigorously using his muscles, heart, tendons, ligaments, bones and joints on a regular basis will need more protein than one who is just roaming around a pasture.

A middle-ground approach for working horses is to shoot for at least a 12% total ration protein level for horses in light work and perhaps 14% to 16% for more moderate-to-heavy work. To get this, you can feed alfalfa hay and a 10% or 12% grain mix in roughly

During exercise, muscle tissue is damaged to some extent, requiring protein for repair.

equal amounts or use mixed alfalfa and grass hay with a higher protein grain mix (14% to 16%, depending on hay quality). If you are feeding only grass hay, you will need a protein supplement.

Protein supplements

Protein is expensive. Fortunately, since we are sticking with the relatively conservative recommendations for protein level, you won't have to feed too much. The familiar Calf-Manna (Manna Pro) at 25% protein and a product called Amino Fac 41 (Uckele Animal Health Corp) with 41% protein, are two supplements we especially like. Both contain 3% lysine and a blend of vegetable protein (soybean) and milk protein.

Milk protein is among the most easily digested by all animals and contains an excellent variety of amino acids. How much you need to feed to reach the targeted protein level will depend on exactly what your base diet is. We recommend you consult your veterinarian, agricultural extension agent, equine nutritionist or a feed company representative for specific advice.

As an example, if your horse daily eats 10 kg (22 pounds) of hay and grain combined and is in moderately heavy use, you may want to achieve a 15% protein level. If you feed a 12% protein high-quality mixed hay and a 14% protein grain mix, your ration will have an overall protein content of 13%. You will still need to supply 2 percent, or 200 grams, of protein (10 kg x 2% = .20 kg = 200 grams).

Calf-Manna supplies 113.5 grams of protein per pound while Amino Fac 21 has 186.14. The horse will therefore need about 1.75 pounds of Calf-Manna per day or 1.07 pounds of Amino Fac 41.

Always introduce protein supplements very, very gradually, as many horses will develop some increased intestinal gas and distention if a rapid change is made. The soybean (see Chapter 11) is likely the problem here. At different times, our veterinary consultants have fed powdered skim milk and milk-and-egg human protein supplements in equivalent amounts without this problem, but the same horses needed time to adapt to either product.

As a quick note on older horses, a 12% protein diet should be maintained and should be of the highest quality you can get. Digestive upset is often more of a problem in older horses. Your first concern will always be to feed something the horse can tolerate well.

If the tolerated ration still falls short on protein, you may want to consider the milk-and-egg protein products mentioned above. We used milk-and-egg protein from the health-food store, which contains 21 grams of protein per ounce (one tablespoon). Since these products are more digestible (nearly 100%) than vegetable protein, such as soy, you can feed less.

As little as 40 to 50 grams per day in the older horse's diet may show up quickly as improved coat quality. The whey (milk portion) may also have the added advantage of helping improve immune function. ▣

For contact information on specific products mentioned, please see page 204.

7

The Alfalfa Debate

If you could take a survey of horses regarding their opinion on alfalfa, the results would be unanimous — they love it! However, replies from nutritionists would not be as clear cut.

Alfalfa is the oldest cultivated crop in the United States. While we have the Native Americans to thank for introducing us to corn, the favor was returned several-fold when colonists brought alfalfa to American shores in 1736. The known history of alfalfa, however, far predates even Columbus. There are references to alfalfa being fed to animals as far back as 490 B.C. Though it originated in the Middle East, alfalfa is now grown worldwide.

The alfalfa plant is actually more closely related to clover than to grass. Being a legume, it concentrates nitrogen more heavily than grasses, which is what gives alfalfa its higher protein content than most grass hays.

The leaves of the alfalfa plant are arranged in groups of three (sometimes more) on the stem of the plant. Mature plants have from five to 25 stems and reach a height of 15 to 25 inches. **Alfalfa does well in many areas but prefers a well-drained soil, neutral pH and plenty of water.**

The nutritional value of alfalfa is located in the leaves. Plants are most nutritious when hay is harvested at the bud stage, before it has bloomed. If harvesting is done beyond this stage, the hay will contain more fiber and less protein and be less digestible.

When selecting alfalfa hay, look for a bright green color. The hay should be highly fragrant and "sweet" smelling. A high proportion of leaves to stems is desirable.

Make hay while the sun shines

For many people, the decision to feed alfalfa is virtually a foregone conclusion. In many areas, it is either the best or the only hay available for horses; grass hays are simply too "pricey" or in short supply. **When feeding alfalfa, or any hay, the first consideration must be if it was baled properly**, which has more to do with the hay itself than the farmer.

Alfalfa has a higher moisture content than grass hays. This means it must be thoroughly air and sun-dried before it is baled, which requires the cooperation of the weather. Deciding to cut and cure alfalfa must be to farmers like washing our car is to us — do it, and you can bet it's going to rain! Baling it with too high a moisture content leads to excessive heating and molding, both of which greatly decrease the nutritional value. Fortunately, the ability to get three, four or more cuttings from a field of alfalfa over the season usually means enough will get properly cured.

Bale-buying tips

Before purchasing, examine the bales for excessive loss of color or an "off" smell. Pick up several bales to make sure they are fairly uniform in weight. Heavier bales were probably too wet when put up and are likely to be moldy. Before accepting a large load, open several bales (buy them first if you have to). The hay should come apart in flakes easily and shake out freely. If centers are matted together, they have probably molded. If bales are very heavy and the centers feel hotter than the outside, the hay has not completely cured. Avoid these bales (although they will probably look and smell great), since you cannot predict if they will eventually mold.

Nutrient content

Energy — Alfalfa is the most energy-rich of all the hays. National Research Council (NRC) estimates an average digestible-energy content of 0.94 megacalories per pound of sun-cured alfalfa hay, but less than 0.75 for most common grass hays. **This means you can feed about 10 percent less alfalfa hay than grass hay while main-**

All hays must be properly sun-dried before baling, but because of its higher moisture content, alfalfa hay requires more curing time.

taining your horse at the same weight. This is a plus economically and should be considered when comparing the price of alfalfa and grass hays. Unfortunately, this feature makes alfalfa a poor choice for overweight horses, since one of the major problems you face in trying to keep weight off a horse is trying to feed him enough to avoid boredom or a sense of hunger.

Protein — The protein content of alfalfa hays is much higher than grass hays, higher, in fact, than grains as well. **Alfalfa is also a good source of the essential amino acid lysine.** (An essential amino acid is one that must be provided in the diet because the horse's body cannot manufacture it.) **Lysine has been shown to be critical for growth as well as for all body functions.**

The protein content of alfalfa is so great (average 17 to 20 percent or even higher) that some people condemn it as "harmful." The fact is, there is no evidence that confirms protein intakes in this range are harmful to horses. (An exception might be endurance horses, where high protein intakes may interfere with the horse's ability to handle the high protein turnover that occurs during prolonged exercise. However, even in these horses, most experts agree that the old recommended protein level of eight to 10 percent is not adequate.)

Protein has been blamed for many things, from poor performance to "overloading the kidneys" to orthopedic problems in growing

Alfalfa Myths

MYTH #1 *First cutting is not good for horses.*

Although a commonly held opinion, there is really no basis for this. First-cutting hays are among the richest in all nutrients. About the only problem commonly encountered with first-cutting hays is they tend to have the highest percentage of weeds. However, this is not always the case, and it is a mistake to turn down first-cutting hay on the impression that it is "no good" or unsafe.

MYTH #2 *Alfalfa is too "rich."*

You hear this comment made frequently, but no one really defines "rich." Although alfalfa is "richer" in protein and digestible energy than other hays, this is not necessarily bad. It does mean that you should always make the addition of alfalfa to the diet gradually, allowing the microorganisms of the intestinal tract sufficient time to adjust. An abrupt change to alfalfa can lead to some bloating and loose green manure in some horses, although rarely anything more serious.

Alfalfa is also "rich" in calcium, but it's "poor" in phosphorus. Calcium and phosphorus should be fed in a correct ratio in the diet, which means that either a phosphorus-rich feed, such as grain or bran, or a phosphorus supplement will be necessary to balance out the alfalfa in your horse's diet.

MYTH #3 *Alfalfa can damage the kidneys.*

This myth may have its roots in the higher protein content or the high calcium level of alfalfa. However, there is absolutely no evidence that alfalfa is damaging to a horse's kidneys. In fact, horses have an extremely low incidence of kidney problems of any type and, given the large numbers of horses that happily consume alfalfa all their lives, you can be sure that if it was causing kidney problems, this would have been confirmed medically by now.

horses, such as epiphysitis. However, again, there is no supporting evidence for these accusations.

In fact, the tide is turning, and nutritionists are beginning to emphasize that inadequate total protein intake — or, at least, inadequate intake of high-quality proteins — is likely to be at the root of many common problems, including growth-oriented bone disorders that had once been blamed on too much protein! The bottom line is that the high protein content of alfalfa is a point in its favor, not a drawback.

ALFALFA DOES WELL IN MANY AREAS BUT
PREFERS A WELL-DRAINED SOIL, NEUTRAL
PH AND PLENTY OF WATER.

Mineral Levels

Calcium: Alfalfa hay is notoriously high in calcium, containing 1.24 percent calcium on the average in sun-cured, mid-bloom hay, compared to about 0.12 to 0.24 percent for most common grass hays, a few going as high as 0.3 to 0.4 percent calcium. **No horse being maintained on alfalfa hay should ever receive a supplement containing calcium** (with the possible exception being some stages of pregnancy, lactation and growth).

Unfortunately, this high calcium level can cause problems, at least theoretically. Calcium levels in the blood are tightly controlled to remain in a narrow "normal" range by the actions of a hormone called parathormone. This same hormone controls the amount of calcium that is absorbed from the intestinal tract, decreasing absorption when levels become high.

Unfortunately, this system is not perfect. Nevertheless, it has been estimated that calcium intakes of up to five to six times the required amount can be tolerated by horses if their total intake of the mineral phosphorus is adequate. A 1,000-pound horse should receive about 14 grams of phosphorus per day. So, **it doesn't matter how much extra calcium the alfalfa provides if the horse's phosphorus needs are being met.**

The high calcium content of alfalfa makes it ideal for pregnant and lactating mares, as well as growing horses. Again, this must be balanced by adequate phosphorus intake for proper bone growth to occur.

Phosphorus: For calcium and phosphorus to work properly, they should be present in the diet at a ratio of about 1.5 to 1.8 parts calcium to one part of phosphorus (Ca:Phos = 1.5:1.0 to 1.8:1.0). As we saw above, alfalfa more than fulfills the horse's need for calcium. However, it is extremely low in phosphorus, with an average of only about 0.22 percent phosphorus in sun-cured mid-bloom hay.

Grain can help balance the calcium-phosphorus ratio. Corn has a phosphorus content of about 0.27 percent; barley and oats, about 0.34 percent (NRC figures). This means one pound of corn will contain 1.23 grams of phosphorus; other grains about 1.5 grams of phosphorus per kilogram. Our 1,000-pound horse would need 11.4 pounds of corn or 9.02 pounds of oats to supply the additional phosphorus he needs. This is no problem for horses who are in work, but for horses who are being maintained on a hay-only diet, you will either need to supplement the phosphorus level or switch to a 50:50 mixture of grass and alfalfa hay, which has a correct Ca:Phos ratio.

Magnesium: Judging only by the NRC's reported magnesium level, alfalfa hay should contain sufficient magnesium to meet most horses' needs. Unfortunately, we find the situation is a little more complicated. Magnesium and calcium are absorbed by the same intestinal

Alfalfa hay is stored in covered hay barns in dry areas like Arizona.

Alfalfa is a good choice for mares with foals alongside, as long as you supplement phosphorus.

system. **However, the horse's system is geared to absorb calcium, and magnesium absorption will suffer in the presence of an excess of calcium, which is found in alfalfa.** The situation is worse in some areas of the country where calcium levels in the water ("hard," untreated water) can be hundreds of times higher than magnesium.

There is not much written in this country regarding possible magnesium deficiency under these circumstances, and blood tests can be deceiving, since most of the body's magnesium is either bound up in bone or located inside the cells, not floating in the blood. Nevertheless, some veterinarians have seen typical magnesium-related problems (muscle pain and cramping, poor exercise tolerance) in horses on high-alfalfa diets, and research in other countries has confirmed this can happen.

A ratio of calcium to magnesium of from 1.5:1 to 2.0:1 is needed to prevent magnesium-related work problems. This level of magnesium will not be available from standard feeds. The best advice at this point seems to be that if your horse has problems with poor exercise tolerance and/or muscle pain, cramping or tying-up, you should sit down with your veterinarian, an equine nutritionist or a feed-company consultant and explore the ways you can use available magnesium supplements to boost your horse's magnesium intake up to a level that equals the above ratios.

Trace minerals: Trace minerals (copper, zinc, manganese, sulfur, iron, selenium, cobalt) are required in very low levels. Don't let this fool you, though. Trace minerals are also present in low levels in feeds, meaning they are not all that easy to come by. Despite the low requirements, inadequate intake of trace minerals can have disastrous consequences. Metabolic bone disease in growing horses (including OCD — osteochondrosis dessicans), anemia, impaired growth, weakness of tendons, improper functioning of the immune system and metabolic abnormalities in the processing of carbohydrates, fats and protein are among the potential effects of insufficient intake of trace minerals.

While alfalfa shows up in the plus column for many of the major nutrients discussed above, it actually checks out at below-average levels for trace minerals when compared to grains and the grass hays. If your horse's diet contains a high percentage of alfalfa, consult your veterinarian or equine nutritionist about the advisability of providing a trace-mineral supplement to your horse and exactly how much to use. Since the amount required is fairly small, it is possible to overdo it and cause problems. This is one situation where more is definitely not necessarily better. ☐

8

Grains A to Z

*Deciding whether your horse truly needs
grain is your first step.
Then you decide which grain best meets his needs.*

G rains are classified as energy feeds or "concentrates." They contain more energy (calories) per given weight and volume than do forages or hays. Other feeds, such as wheat bran, rice bran, brewer's by-products, molasses and high-energy/high-protein supplements like Calf-Manna also contribute, but these are fed in limited amounts. The primary reason for feeding grain is to provide the horse with calories for maintaining or gaining weight, pregnancy, lactating (making milk), growth, breeding or exercise.

Grains are also used, to a limited extent, to balance the mineral and vitamin composition in the diet. Grains are a better source of B vitamins than hays and supply more phosphorus, generally, than hays. However, they may do little to contribute to trace-mineral levels in the diet, and they contain little or no vitamin A, E, D or C and have no advantage in the major mineral categories (such as potassium and calcium).

Grain Conversion

The easiest way to feed by weight instead of volume without resorting to buying a scale is to use a grain scoop calibrated in quart measures. The following conversions then apply:

- 1 quart oats = 1 pound
- 1 quart corn = approximately 2 pounds
- 1 quart sweet feed = approximately 1.5 pounds
- 1 quart dry bran = 0.5 pounds

Horses in moderate-to-heavy work usually require grain to maintain their weight and energy levels.

Many people also think of grains as high-protein feeds. The fact is that grains often contain no more protein than good-quality hay, plus the quality of the protein may be poor. In the final analysis, the major contribution of grains to the horse's diet is in terms of energy/calories.

Which horses need grain?

As a general rule, grains are not needed in a horse's diet unless the horse is unable to maintain his normal body weight on hay or pasture alone. If the horse is eating all the hay and grass he can possibly eat but still losing weight, or not maintaining weight at an ideal healthy level, a more concentrated source of calories is needed. Grain is usually not needed for horses in the following categories: adult horse at maintenance (no work), adult horse in light work, breeding stallions when not actively breeding, all ponies and breeding mares when not pregnant or for the first third to half of pregnancy (assuming the mare is in good body condition to begin with). Grain will usually be required for horses in moderate (over one hour per day on a regular basis), heavy or endurance work, for mares in the last half of pregnancy, for lactating mares, for growing horses, for stallions during the breeding season and for any horse who is not holding weight well. The best indicator of when to begin feeding grain is body condition. There are rules of thumb and complicated equations you can use to calculate the horse's predicted energy needs and diet, but in the end the most reliable indicator is still how well the horse looks — how well he is holding his weight. The horseman's eye is mightier than the calculator!

A common mistake made is to use the size of the horse's abdomen ("belly") to judge how fat the horse is or, conversely, how thin. While horses at both extremes of abdominal size (huge, swinging belly versus severe tucked-up, fish-like appearance) are obviously too fat or too thin, abdominal size is influenced by factors other than amount of body fat.

Horses on a hay-only diet tend to have larger abdomens because the diet is bulkier and harder to digest. Excess gas and fluid from inefficient digestion, as well as excessive fluid and undigested feed in heavily parasite-infested horses, also make the abdomen large. It is possible for a horse to have a big belly but have prominent ribs and top line, as well. Such a horse is actually malnourished and underweight, despite the pot belly.

Similarly, as a horse progresses through an exercise program, his abdominal muscles will strengthen. This leads to improved support of the intestinal tract and a tighter, more streamlined look to the abdomen. A check of other areas of the body, however, may show the ribs are well covered with a thin layer of fat and the muscles of the back, hindquarters and chest are well developed and prominent. This horse may look thinner than the one with the big abdomen, but he is actually in better condition and probably weighs more, since muscle weighs more than fat, fluid or gas.

Commercial mixes and sweet feeds

Commercial grain mixes for horses, usually in the form of a sweet feed (moistened and held together with molasses), are more expensive than plain grains but have some advantages. When using a sweet mix with a guaranteed analysis, the major and minor mineral and protein contents will be stable from batch to batch. This may be accomplished through natural ingredients or by the addition of supplemental levels of minerals.

Protein content is adjusted using such things as soybean meal or alfalfa meal — in a few cases, even milk proteins. This usually results in a better-quality protein overall and a vast improvement in the level of essential amino acids.

Unfortunately, while the protein supplement may be a good choice, the base grains are sometimes not of the quality you would get if you were purchasing the single grains alone.

To assure the quality of your sweet feed, buy only animal feed with a nutritional breakdown listed on the label. Also, take the time to inspect the quality of a sample of the feed. **Kernels of grain should be fat and smooth. There should be far more kernel present than husk or "shell."** Empty hulls and bits of corn cob have little nutritional value. Inspect the feed at the mill. If you find unidentifiable components in there, ask for an explanation.

Sweet feeds are also often vitamin-fortified. This is a plus, but only if you realize that **many vitamins have a short shelf life, especially when mixed into a moist feed**. The bag should come stamped with an expiration or "use before" date. If it does not, don't choose it just for the vitamin content.

You may also call the manufacturer to ask if the vitamins added to the feed have been stabilized. There are various processing techniques for vitamins that will increase their shelf life, although as you might suspect, these vitamins will cost more and lower the manufacturer's profit margin.

Processing grains

Grains can be processed to make them more digestible (rolling/crushing, crimping, cracking and steaming). The purpose of processing is to crack through the tough outer shell of the grain to expose the nutritious inner portion. This exposes the grain better to digestive enzymes and fluids in the intestinal tract, for increased yield in terms of energy and calories.

Storing grain

Grains should be kept in an area that is dry, as free of dust as possible, not exposed to sun and not subject to extremes of heat. Containers with lids should be used. Large trash cans or specially designed grain bins, preferably metal for ease of cleaning, are ideal.

Use containers that will hold approximately one to two weeks' worth of grain. Storage for longer than this time, especially with sweet feeds, can result in loss of vitamin content, rancidity of the fat portion of the feed or mold formation — the latter especially if containers are tight and the weather is hot and humid.

After finishing a week or two's worth of grain, remove any remaining traces of grain before dumping in your next supply. Round containers are a little easier to empty and clean since the grain does not become lodged into corners. Containers need not be washed out every time they are emptied but should be cleaned with a dust brush and emptied completely.

THE MAJOR CONTRIBUTION OF GRAINS TO THE HORSE'S DIET IS IN TERMS OF ENERGY/CALORIES.

If residue begins to build up on the walls of the container (usually when sweet feeds are used), you can wash this out using hot water and dish soap. But, don't overdo it, as residue can leave a soapy taste in the container that the grain will pick up. This is especially true with plastic containers. We recommend Dawn dish soap in grain containers, since it is the easiest to rinse out and least likely to leave a soapy taste in plastic. Containers should be thoroughly dried before refilling — towel them out and leave them exposed to air and, if possible, sun for 30 minutes to an hour. If your container has a hinged lid, carefully check the hinges for trapped grain or residue.

There are special considerations for storage of corn. Cracked corn quickly loses its vitamin content and should not be stored for more than two weeks after cracking. (While cracked corn is often added to sweet feeds, additional vitamins are usually added to the mixture.) **Grain should not be stored in tightly sealed containers as this favors the development of condensation.** If you are using plastic trash cans as grain containers, store the corn with the lid removed, inside its original bag (if it's paper; if the bag is plastic, dump the corn out first), with a fine screen weighed down by rocks or bricks on top of the container. (A window screen works well — anything to prevent rodent access.)

Types of grains

OATS: Oats are the most popular grain for horses because they are widely available and usually easily digested.

■ *Protein content varies from 9% to 12.5%, with the heaviest, plumpest oats being the best source of protein. However, the protein in oats is deficient in essential amino acids.*

■ *B vitamin levels are quite low and cannot be relied upon as a supplemental source of B vitamins in horses with increased B vitamin needs.*

■ *Oats contain little calcium (hay is the major source of this mineral) and only a moderate amount of phosphorus.*

■ *Oats contain low-to-moderate amounts of magnesium, manganese, copper and zinc. Iron levels, as in all common horse feeds, are more than adequate.*

CORN: Corn is usually well accepted by horses; many are especially fond of dried corn that is still on the cob.

■ *Corn provides twice the calories of an equal amount of oats on a volume basis.*

■ *Top protein content for corn is around 9%, and it is extremely low in essential amino acids, especially lysine.*

■ *Phosphorus level is lower than in oats, as are levels of all important vitamins and minerals.*

■ *Even iron levels in corn will usually fall below the estimated requirement, although other hays and grains easily make up the difference.*

BARLEY: Barley grains are small and have a thick hull, making them somewhat unpalatable. However, barley can be boiled, cracked or rolled to improve palatability.

■ *Barley contains slightly more energy and protein than oats. Barley also is still deficient in essential amino acids.*

■ *The mineral-and-vitamin composition is similar to that of other grains.*

SORGHUM (MILO): Sorghum is widely used as a horse grain in areas where other concentrates are not readily available. Sorghum is a small, dense grain made more palatable by processing.

■ *Used as a substitute for the corn portion of a ration, sorghum contains an energy content roughly between that of barley and corn but higher than oats.*

WHEAT AND RYE: These grains are less easily digested by most horses. Wheat and rye may be fed to horses at a rate of no more than 10% to 20% of the grain ration. Processing improves digestibility and palatability, and is a must for these grains.

■ *Wheat and rye contain more energy than oats or barley, and roughly the same to slightly more than corn.*

■ *Protein content is similar to oats and, again, both are deficient in essential amino acids.*

■ *Vitamin-and-mineral composition is also similar to that of other grains, except that wheat and rye are a source of vitamin E — a hard-to-come-by vitamin in many common equine feeds.*

Rodent control is a must

Mice, rats and other wildlife can spread disease or even contaminate the grain area with botulism toxin if they should die in the area. Adult animals are easy to spot and remove, but abandoned litters may not be so obvious and are a potential source of contamination.

Barn cats are a natural and excellent way to control rodents. Traps can also be used and checked daily for victims, which must then be disposed of immediately.

Poisonous baits are not a good idea, since the animal may not get far enough away before the poison takes effect and will then die somewhere in the barn — usually in a spot difficult, if not impossible, to find!

Cats are a cost-effective 24-hour-a-day rodent control.

Weight versus volume

The rule of thumb for feeding grain:
- no grain for horses at maintenance (finished growing, not in work, not pregnant or breeding, at a good body weight);
- 0.5 to 1.0 pound per 100 pounds of body weight for light work;
- 1.0 to 1.5 pounds per 100 pounds for moderate work;
- 1.5 to 2.0 pounds per 100 pounds for heavy work.

By knowing how much you are feeding on a weight basis, it is easier to determine what adjustments you should make if your horse's status changes — i.e., if you increase or decrease work, if the horse is pregnant, and so forth. You will also be able to see if your horse is an "easy keeper" (does well on less-than-average amounts of grain) or a "hard keeper" (needs more grain than average to maintain weight).

Tips for feeding grain

Most horses will adjust well to the addition of grain in their diet, or to a change in grains, if it is done gradually. Introduction of grain, or changes in grain, should be done at a rate of no greater than one

Recommendations for selection and processing of common feed grains

Type of grain	Desirable characteristics	Recommended processing
Oats	Clean. Dust free. Fat kernels. Bushel weight over 32 pounds. No or few free hulls in bag.	Feed whole, unprocessed oats to normal adult horses. Crimping and rolling/steam rolling improve digestion for very young or old horses. "Racehorse oats" have had the fibrous ends removed, which increases the energy and protein content, but makes the feed more expensive.
Corn	Fat kernels. Clean, free of mold or dust.	Should be fed crimped, cracked or coarsely ground.
Barley	Clean, plump, free from dust or mold, no empty hulls.	Crushed, cracked or rolled for improved palatability. May also be fed after boiling.
Sorghum	Clean, plump, free from dust or mold, no empty hulls.	Cracked, crushed or coarsely ground. Soaking recommended.
Wheat	Clean, plump, free from dust or mold, no empty hulls.	Soak first if feeding whole. Cracked/crimped best.
Rye	Clean, plump, free from dust or mold, no empty hulls.	Store for two months before feeding. Cracked, crushed or steam-rolled.

to two pounds per day, in divided feedings. Allow the horse to stabilize at this level for two to three days, then increase or change/substitute again, at the same rate (one to two pounds per change). Hay consumption should remain the same.

Some horses require extra grain only when working. Feeding it daily, regardless of work, may result in too great a weight gain. In those cases, omit grain on days when the horse does not work.

When attempting weight gain or loss by manipulating the grain ration, begin with one- to two-pound adjustments in the grain, waiting at least a week to assess the effect of the change.

Ponies should rarely, if ever, be fed grain. Their metabolism is different from that of a horse. They are more prone to obesity, digestive upsets and founder when given grains. If overall nutrition is a concern because of poor-quality hay, you would be better off going with an alfalfa-based complete feed or a high-fiber low-calorie commercial feed. **PH**

9

Feeding Bran

*Fed through the centuries as a special feed for tired
horses, or once a week as a laxative,
bran has a history of being misunderstood.*

B ran is an economic, palatable and highly nutritious addition to a horse's diet. When fed as recommended, it is safe and a good insurance policy against a wide variety of possible nutritional inadequacies in traditional equine diets. Bran is the tough outer coating, or "shell," found on grains. In the process of milling grains to make flour, this outer shell is cracked and removed. The result is a fine, flaky, almost powdered concentrate of the grain. Depending upon the milling process used, brans will contain varying amounts of other grain products, including flour.

Wheat bran is the traditional product fed to horses and other livestock. Lately, however, rice bran has become more available and is also an appropriate feed for horses.

Why feed bran?

Everybody knows you feed bran as a laxative, right? Wrong. Bran acts as a laxative for humans, whose foods are generally highly processed and very low in fiber. **However, for a horse, the fiber content of bran is actually fairly low — only 10% fiber compared to 20% to 30% for hays, 40% for straws.**

There is one characteristic of bran that makes it helpful in preventing impactions. **It has the ability to hold a fairly large amount of water and it therefore helps to keep water in the horse's**

This picture was taken five minutes after adding water to the bran and covering the bucket. The water is not entirely absorbed.

intestine and prevent the manure from becoming too dried out. This is why bran is usually fed wet, as a mash. Feeding bran dry can have an opposite effect. The bran will draw water from the intestinal contents, even from the body. If the horse is not drinking enough, free water in the intestine will be decreased to below normal, drying out the manure and causing other problems for the horse.

Another common myth about bran is that it is low in nutrition. The facts do not support this. Compared to oats, bran has at least as much energy (calories) and 50 percent more protein, more of the essential (necessary in the diet) amino acid lysine, and is a rich source of many minerals. Compared to timothy hay, bran has 1.6 times the protein and 1.66 times the energy (calories). The Nutrient Chart on page 202 in our appendix compares the energy, protein and major mineral content of bran to oats and common hays.

Bran is also very rich in B vitamins. **The fact is, bran has so much to offer nutritionally, it is classified by the National Research Council as an "energy food" — not a roughage.** Let's look at some of the nutrients in bran and their value to the horse.

Calcium

Calcium is one mineral that is in very low supply in bran. If you are feeding straight alfalfa hay, this is a plus, since the alfalfa already contains an excessive amount of calcium. **However, if feeding a mixed hay or grass hay, you should add calcium to the bran to increase total calcium and also bring the calcium-to-phosphorus ratio (Ca:Ph) into balance.** For mixed-hay diets, add one ounce of ground limestone (readily available from feed stores); for grass hay diets, add two ounces.

Phosphorus

Bran contains large amounts of phosphorus. A one-pound serving of wheat bran (two quarts) will provide 11.3 grams of phosphorus.

An inactive 1,000-pound horse only needs a total of 15.3 grams per day. The maximum safe intake of phosphorus (on a long-term basis) for the same horse is one percent of the total ration, assuming the horse is getting enough calcium. The 1,000-pound horse at maintenance (i.e., no work) needs a minimum of 10 pounds of hay per day to maintain his body weight. This allows for a total daily safe intake of phosphorus of 45.4 grams.

If you were feeding alfalfa, 10 pounds would give him 10.89 grams of phosphorus. Ten pounds of timothy would provide 9.08 grams of phosphorus. You can therefore safely feed up to about three pounds of bran per day (six quarts), which is really about all the horse could manage to consume at one sitting.

BRAN USED FOR HORSES SHOULD CONTAIN LITTLE, OR NO, FLOUR. FLOUR IS A CONCENTRATED STARCH AND CAN PRODUCE SEVERE DIGESTIVE PROBLEMS FOR HORSES IF IT REACHES THE LARGE INTESTINES.

Note: **The maximal daily allowance of phosphorus for horses in work is still one percent of the total daily ration.** However, since the working horse will require more feed than the horse at maintenance, his total daily phosphorus allowance will increase. For example, a horse consuming 20 pounds per day of alfalfa (about one-third of a medium-size bale) would be allowed 90.8 grams total and could safely be fed six pounds (12 quart scoop measures) of bran, with calcium supplementation.

Grains contain more phosphorus than hays and will provide from 25% to 50% more phosphorus than an equivalent amount of hay.

(Top) Salt and molasses are commonly added to bran mashes. (Middle) One ounce of salt is about a small palmful. (Bottom) You can see we've added enough water to cover the bran. We don't want it too dry or too sloppy.

(For example, oats have 0.34%, compared to alfalfa's 0.24% phosphorus.) A horse receiving 10 pounds of oats and 10 pounds of alfalfa hay per day should receive a maximum of about 4.5 pounds of bran (nine quart-size scoops) per day to remain within safe phosphorus intake, adding additional limestone for calcium.

We've gone into some detail on the calcium and phosphorus picture because **long-term intake of excessive phosphorus can produce bone abnormalities, even when calcium intake is adequate.** However, most people feed bran much below the recommended maximum amounts here, and only on an occasional (once or twice a week) basis, not daily over months and months. Unless you feed more than the recommended amount or fail to supplement calcium when needed, bran is perfectly safe.

Magnesium

Magnesium is an important mineral in energy metabolism and muscle contraction, as well as the function of the heart muscle. **Pregnant mares and horses in work require extra magnesium.**

A total dietary level of 0.18% magnesium is recommended for horses in work. Alfalfa meets this need, but grass hays do not. Grains are also low (oats 0.14%) in magnesium. Furthermore, addition of fat to the diet and possibly excess calcium may decrease the absorption of magnesium, creating a shortage in the horse. Irritability and a tendency toward muscle cramping/tying-up is the result. Brans are a rich supplemental source of magnesium.

Copper

Copper is important for prevention of anemia and in the formation of strong and normal joints and tendons. The NRC (National Research Council) recommends a copper level of 10.0 ppm (parts per million) in the feed. Brans contain this minimal recommended amount. However, since recent research indicates the copper level needed to prevent joint deformities or abnormalities in foals may be as much as four times higher than the NRC requirements, **we recommend that pregnant mares and foals receiving bran as a significant, regular component of their diet be supplemented with a copper supplement or a rich natural source of copper, such as molasses.**

Manganese

Manganese is a mineral that most people have never heard of, but it plays a critical role in the formation and health of normal joints. The NRC recommends a level of 40.0 ppm (mg/kg of diet) of manganese. Grass hays are very good sources of manganese, but alfalfa and the grains are borderline to low in this important mineral.

Brans are an excellent source of manganese and the perfect complement to a horse receiving alfalfa hay only or a grain and alfalfa diet.

Selenium

Selenium is a familiar mineral to most people because of its widely publicized connection with tying-up. Deficiencies of this mineral are also associated with reproductive problems.

Selenium is concentrated in brans to a much higher level than in whole grains or hays. In fact, **daily use of bran could eliminate the need for selenium supplements. However, selenium content varies widely depending on soil conditions**. For this reason, if you

Bran fully expanded in water has the consistency of cooked oatmeal.

live in an area (or get feed from an area) that is known to be either high or low in selenium, you should first consult your veterinarian and the local state agricultural extension agent for information about the selenium content in brans locally, as well as for guidelines on the safety of feeding bran and any other supplement.

Zinc

Zinc is important to the function of many enzyme systems in the body. It affects the health of the eyes, skin, hair, bone, glands and many other organs. Zinc has also been determined to be important in the prevention of bone and joint disease in foals. The NRC recommends a zinc level of 40 ppm in feeds. Researchers in bone and joint disease suggest a level as high as 90 ppm may be optimal for prevention of those problems. **Horses tolerate zinc very well, with a wide margin of safety.** Wheat bran is an excellent source of zinc, with a level of 98 ppm. The zinc content of rice bran is about equivalent to that in the common hays and grains.

B vitamins

B vitamins play many important roles in the body. They are critical to normal production of energy from foods, formation of blood and normal functioning of the nervous system.

The horse's main source of B vitamins is assumed to be from the micro-organisms inhabiting his intestinal tract. They manufacture

B vitamins that are then absorbed by the horse. However, stress of any sort increases the requirements for B vitamins, while anything that interferes with the normal, optimal function of the intestinal tract could decrease the available supply. Even the NRC (which is very conservative in these matters) recognizes that some B vitamins (i.e., thiamine) should be supplemented in working horses.

Bran and sand

Sand impaction is a real problem in many areas of the United States where quality hay or pasture is scarce and horses are turned out to browse on sandy soils. Veterinarians dealing with this problem have varying opinions on the benefit of feeding bran in preventing colic. However, all would agree that daily feeding of small amounts of bran is not likely to have a significant effect on moving sand through the intestinal tract.

On the other hand, horses who are regularly fed a sufficient amount of bran, preferably as a mash, do have an increased ability to mobilize the sand along the intestinal tract, preventing large accumulations that cause impaction requiring surgery.

How much is a "sufficient amount" will depend on the circumstances (i.e., size of horse, other components of diet, amount of sand being consumed). A general guideline would be in the neighborhood of a minimum of two pounds of bran (four quarts) on a daily or every-other-day basis. As in all cases where regular bran is being fed, care must be taken to balance the high intake of phosphorus with additional calcium.

Rice versus wheat bran

The choice of rice versus wheat bran may be made for you, depending upon availability in your area. One difference is that **rice bran contains a high percentage of fat, which limits the amount of time it can be stored**. There are, however, processed rice brans available that are stabilized and that store well for longer periods of time.

Wheat bran has slightly higher energy, protein, calcium, copper, selenium and zinc than rice bran. However, rice bran has more phosphorus, magnesium, manganese and vitamins E and the B group than wheat bran.

Both types of bran are well accepted by horses, especially when prepared in a mash, and there is really no overwhelming reason to choose one over the other unless you are targeting a specific nutritional requirement (i.e., rice bran for magnesium, wheat bran for zinc).

Selecting bran

Bran used for horses should contain little, or no, flour. Flour is a concentrated starch and can produce severe digestive problems for horses if it reaches the large intestines. **Flour contamination of bran can be recognized as a very fine powder, while the bran itself is heavier and more flaky.**

Bran comes bagged, directly from the flour mill. Be sure to specify if you intend to feed the bran to horses when you purchase it from your feed mill. Many flour mills recognize the need to avoid flour contamination of the bran and take care in its processing.

If you open a bag of grain and suspect a significant amount of flour contamination, play it safe and return it to the feed mill. (Remember, the bran was more than likely bagged at the flour mill. Your feed mill can return it there for credit.)

Feeding bran

Although most horses will eat bran dry, some will not because it is too fine. Dry bran is also more likely to cause digestive problems and could be dusty enough to be irritating to the respiratory passages. For these reasons, bran is usually fed as a mash.

The basic ingredients in bran mash are, simply, bran and water. The desired amount of bran is measured into a bucket and hot water is added, enough to cover the bran. Then the mixture is stirred, the bucket covered with a towel, and the bran allowed to soak until the water is absorbed. The end product has a consistency similar to cooked oatmeal.

Bran from different sources may be more fine or coarse than the average. If your mash turns out too wet or too dry, adjust the amount of water used.

Feed the bran when it is comfortably warm. Be sure to stir the mash to check the middle and bottom of the bucket for temperature, as these areas will hold more heat. Bran has a pleasant aroma when warm, and most horses consume it eagerly.

Salt and molasses are commonly added to bran mashes. **Salt brings out the flavor of the bran, making it more appetizing to the horse. Use about one teaspoon of salt per pound of bran.** You can buy liquid molasses from the feed store or grocery, or the dehydrated form (much more economical, and stores well) from feed mills. When using bottled

A sweat scraper makes a great tool for stirring a bran mash.

molasses, add from two to four ounces per pound of bran. For dried molasses, one-eighth to one-quarter pound per pound of bran can be used. **While molasses is added for flavor enhancement, it is actually an excellent complement to the bran since molasses is very high in copper — an area where bran could use a little boost.**

Sliced apples, grated carrots or grains can also be added to the bran mixture, if desired, after the bran has absorbed its water and just before feeding it to the horse.

Guidelines for occasional use of bran

Despite the long-standing history of feeding bran to horses, it remains a somewhat controversial subject among nutritionists and veterinarians. One opinion you may run across is that an occasional (i.e., less than daily) bran feeding does the horse a disservice — that it is a stress to his digestive tract because it is an unaccustomed feed. It is true that *ANY* unaccustomed feed has the potential to cause digestive upset, if only manifested by a change in the manure.

However, it is probably safe to say that thousands, if not millions, of bran mashes have been fed to horses either as "treats" or after a stress such as foaling without any significant problems.

We have heard of stables that have read these precautions about bran and stopped feeding it, feeding instead the occasional beet pulp mash — also an unaccustomed feed. Where the switch was made, stable owners admitted that there had really not been any problems with the bran in the first place. Still, while bran-mash feeding on an occasional basis is highly unlikely to cause any damage, we will admit there are occasions when an individual horse with a less-than-perfectly healthy intestinal tract could be made uncomfortable by bran (or any other unaccustomed feed). If the owner of such a horse wanted to take advantage of bran's benefits, the best course would be to feed a handful or so of dry bran to the horse with each regular graining, to allow the organisms in his intestine to become accustomed to bran.

How much bran to feed

As we've said, an idle horse on a hay-only diet can eat up to three pounds of bran per day in addition to his hay, while an active horse receiving twice as much hay can be fed up to six pounds. Horses on equal amounts of grain and hay in their diet can get up to 4.5 pounds on grain per day safely. (Based on a 1,000-pound horse, 10 pounds feed at maintenance, 20 pounds feed in work.)

Since bran is light but absorbs considerable water in making a mash, the amounts we suggest above are about all the horse could possibly eat at one sitting. Begin with about half the recommended safe amount and work up.

When measuring bran, one quart weighs one-half pound. So, if you have been feeding a cup or two of bran daily, you can see that you are not overdoing it.

Bran is an excellent feed and very economical. ■■

10

Beet Pulp Questions

Is soaking beet pulp before feeding it vital to a horse's health, or is this practice based on an old wives' tale?

"I've always heard that beet pulp should be fed wet, but that if it is wet for too long before you feed it, it ferments and is bad to feed. How should it be fed?
GG/Las Vegas, NV

Beet pulp is one of the most misunderstood feeds, and the manner in which it is fed is important for some horses. **Two key factors in deciding whether to feed it wet or dry are the amount of water the horse drinks and whether beet pulp is part of his regular diet or just being introduced to him.**

Beet pulp does absorb water, and when it does, it swells. Shredded beet pulp can be fed dry safely in moderate amounts (up to one pound) to horses who are used to eating it and when it's fed at the same time as hay and/or grain. This is probably the most common way beet pulp is used when it is being incorporated into the diet on a regular basis.

When beet pulp is being used in larger amounts, without other roughages or grain, soaking with water is advisable. If you have a horse who is not drinking much water (as sometimes happens in cold weather) or whose digestive system is compromised in some way (perhaps by stress from trailering or illness), then soaking beet pulp before feeding it is advised.

Opinions vary as to how much water to use and how long to soak. The temperature of the water, and how this affects soaking time, is also a point of contention. **A middle-ground approach that works** well for many people is to soak the beet pulp in warm water, with or without a handful of salt, in a ratio of 3:1, water to beet pulp, allowing it to sit either overnight or for the time between feedings (roughly eight to 10 hours). Don't allow the beet pulp to soak for longer than about 12 hours (less in hot weather), as it could go bad.

Beet pulp cubes are available in some areas, and these do require special attention. As with hay cubes, feeding large dry cubes increases the chance of "choke" (cube being lodged in the esophagus), even if adequate water is available free choice. Beet pulp cubes should never be fed "as is," even if broken up somewhat; instead, soak them using the same "recipe" and time recommendations as for large feedings of shredded beet pulp, but large cubes may need a 5:1 water-to-pulp ratio.

Readers have expressed concern that when beet pulp expands it can cause colic or even rupture a horse's intestines. While no feed will rupture a horse's intestines, a large amount of dry beet pulp could absorb enough fluid to dry intestinal contents, slowing passage and possibly causing a partial or complete obstruction. This is especially true if the horse does not have adequate water available free choice. By itself, this will not cause the intestines to rupture, but may cause a backup of gas and intestinal contents that could have that result. This is particularly the case in a horse who has not been accustomed to beet pulp, as the organisms in his intestinal tract would not yet be adapted to breaking down and digesting it and would be thrown off balance.

If you are contemplating a complete feed for your horse, many of them use beet pulp as a base and make no mention of feeding it wet.

The key here is moderation and just basic good husbandry. **Beet pulp is very nutritious, containing 1.3 times as much digestible energy as timothy hay, and is safe to feed horses.**

Whenever you introduce a new feed to your horse, be it beet pulp or just a new hay, introduce it slowly, allowing time for him to develop the bacteria necessary for him to digest it. Assuming a healthy horse and adequate water supply, there is no problem with feeding moderate amounts of dry shredded beet pulp. Soaking is preferred if you are using one of the cubed or pelleted beet pulp products or if you're feeding shredded beet pulp without other roughage and grain. ■PH■

11

Soy Intolerance

Soybean meal is one of the most commonly used ingredients in horse feeds and supplements — yet it doesn't agree with many horses.

If your horse has repeated bouts of mild, chronic digestive problems, such as bloating, excessive gas or finicky appetite, suspect a food intolerance, such as soy. Soybean meal is added to sweet-feed mixes, pelleted feeds and extruded feeds to increase the total protein content of the feed. It is also widely used in protein supplements, such as Calf-Manna, and in other supplements. **In general, if there is enough protein in a feed supplement for the protein content to appear on the label, there is a good chance that the feed contains some form of soy.** The amount of soy may vary from batch to batch of a feed, even though the guaranteed total protein content stays the same.

Soybean meal is often used as protein booster for two reasons: It is relatively inexpensive compared to other protein sources, and, if it is processed properly, it is a good source of the essential amino acid lysine.

Although widely used in supplements and feeds, soy can cause digestive problems. In some cases, this is simply a matter of having introduced it into the diet too fast or in too large an amount. In other cases, horses seem to have a true sensitivity or "allergy" to soybean meal.

Symptoms of poor tolerance to soy (or any other element of the diet) could include some degree of bloating (the belly appears bigger than before), increased gas production, possibly increased amount of fluid in the manure ("loose" manure), a dull attitude,

Calf-Manna is an excellent protein supplement, but high in soy.

taking longer than normal to finish eating, louder-than-normal intestinal sounds ("gut rumbling") and possibly mild discomfort, which you can identify by behavior such as looking back at the flanks often and pinning ears when passing gas. Skin problems, such as hives or itching, and even breathing problems can be related to food intolerance in other animals and in people, but have not been directly proven to exist in horses.

We know of one barn where several of the above symptoms developed in five horses when they were switched from a milk-protein-based supplement to a soybean-meal-based supplement. All developed bloating, dullness, increased gas production and a decreased appetite. Symptoms disappeared completely within three days of removing the new supplement and going back to the milk-based product. Three of the five horses were able to eventually adapt to the soybean meal when it was added very slowly to their diet. The other two never did get used to it and had to stay on the milk protein. Interestingly, one of these horses had a history of being a picky eater and leaving behind pellets from her sweet feed. It turned out those pellets were soybean meal — the mare had been smarter than her owners all along. (That same mare loves beet pulp-based pellets, so we couldn't blame the form of the feed.)

The symptoms of soy intolerance are relatively mild and could easily be overlooked. **Most horses can tolerate soy-based products well if introduction is made gradually.** However, this problem could be widespread, possibly because use of this potentially allergenic substance is so common and many young horses are exposed to it at a early age.

If you suspect a soy-intolerance problem, try your horse on straight oats or a homemade sweet feed, which is made by mixing diluted molasses (or reconstituted dried molasses) with the straight oats. If problems disappear, try adding a small amount of corn for a few days (corn could also be poorly tolerated by some horses). If the horse does OK on this mixture, suspect that soy or some other ingredient in your previous feed was the culprit. ■■

12

Horse Food Only, Please

Maybe you've run out of horse feed,
or your horse is hankering for the cows' silage.
Is it OK to feed him some? Usually, NO.

he words, "livestock" and "horse" are not interchangeable
— at least when it comes to feeds. Giving your horse a product designed for another animal could result in serious
health problems. We'll walk you through the major con-
cerns, then give you some guidelines.

If horses and cattle are pastured together, they should be fed in
separate areas.

Silage and haylage

Most horses can't resist the pungent aroma of a high-quality silage or haylage. It is just as nutritious for horses as for cows, and the horse can digest moderate amounts well, too. The problem lies in the risk of botulism. Botulism contamination of these feeds is not uncommon, probably from rodents that become trapped and die in the silo.

Cows are much less susceptible to botulism than horses are because of the arrangement of their digestive tract, with all incoming food sources being fermented in the forestomachs before there is much chance of absorption. You won't be able to tell by odor, appearance or any external indicator if there is botulism contamination. Even having a sample tested wouldn't do much good since the toxin would likely be concentrated in a small pocket(s) in the silo rather than spread and mixed evenly throughout all the contents. Feeding these things to horses is like playing Russian Roulette.

Urea

Urea is a protein byproduct that the organisms in ruminant (cow, sheep, goat) forestomachs can convert into usable protein. The horse (especially older horses) may be able to tolerate and even convert a small amount of urea, but higher levels are extremely toxic. Urea is a common ingredient in other livestock feeds.

Medicated feeds

■ *Antibiotics*: Antibiotics are commonly added to livestock and poultry feeds as they increase growth in these species. However, feeding antibiotics to horses may lead to imbalances in the intestinal organisms and cause digestive upset, diarrhea or colic.

■ *Ionophores*: Ionophores, i.e., Rumensin, are substances related to antibiotics that cause favorable shifts in fermentation in the complicated forestomachs of ruminants. They are also used to control coccidial infections in fowl. Ionophores are EXTREMELY toxic to horses.

■ *Supplement Blocks*: Feeds are not the only source of toxic or inappropriate substances for horses. Supplement blocks and licks designed for use by other livestock can be the greatest hazard of all.

Urea and ionophores are common ingredients and in very concentrated amounts — far more than would be found in grain mixes. Many of these blocks also contain molasses to encourage consumption, making the horse even more likely to take in a toxic dose.

The mineral mix in supplement blocks is also often inappropriate for horses. Blocks for cattle contain varying amounts of calcium and phosphorus and are often designed to complement a specific diet or stage of lactation/pregnancy. The trace-mineral profile of the block is also not necessarily the best for horses. In particular, copper levels are likely to be way too low.

■ *Fumonisin*: Fumonisin is the toxin produced by corn contaminated with the mold *Fusarium moniliforme*. This mold is found throughout the Corn Belt, and much of the corn grown in the United States contains it. Moldy corn poisoning in horses can occur at very, very low levels of the toxin, much lower than is toxic to other farm animals. This toxin can cause digestive or kidney problems and in the worst scenario results in leucoencephalomalacia — a fancy medical term that literally means the brain of the horse melts away! Needless to say, this is fatal, and there is no known treatment. Most equine feed mills use a test for the toxin to guard against use of contaminated corn in horse feeds, but feeds for other animals and poultry could contain corn screenings (fine pieces of corn) with toxic levels of the toxin.

■ *Coccidiostats*: Feeds designed for poultry often contain drugs to control parasitism by coccidia. Some of these chemicals are toxic to horses (i.e., amprolium).

■ *Cow hay vs. horse hay:* While high-producing dairy cows often enjoy only the choicest, most nutritious of hays, other classes of cows and other types of livestock can get by successfully on much lower-quality hay than can be safely fed to horses. Hays that are excessively heavy, tightly matted together, produce clouds of "dust" or have an obviously musty odor contain molds can often be safely consumed by cattle. But, molds produce a variety of toxins that can produce health problems in horses.

Particularly dangerous are hays that contain sweet clover. Sweet clover is a high-moisture plant that is difficult to dry and cure properly. As a result, it almost always contains mold. The molds can convert a chemical normally present in the clover (and harmless in its natural form) into the substance dicoumarol. This is the "blood thinner" otherwise known as "Coumadin" — used to treat blood clots and some other problems in people (and sometimes navicular disease in horses) and also the active ingredient in some rat poisons. Dicoumarol can produce abortion, bleeding into the placenta and heavy uterine bleeding in pregnant mares, foals born dead from hemorrhages, and bleeding problems in nonpregnant mares and male horses, as well.

Read the label

If you are contemplating buying a product for your horse that is not specifically labeled for use in horses, get a tag/ingredients list and avoid the following:

- *Ionophores.*
- *Monensin (trade name Rumensin).*
- *Lasalocid (Bovatec).*
- *The term "medicated" usually refers to antibiotics such as the -cillins, -mycins and -cyclines (look for any word ending with these). Also avoid any sulfa substances.*
- *The terms "starter" or "growth promotant" (refers to antibiotics or other chemicals added).*
- *Corn screenings.*
- *Urea.*
- *"Biuret" is a urea-related substance. May also be listed as "nonprotein nitrogen."*

Recommendations

Protect your horse from harmful feed additives by purchasing only feeds/grains that are marked as for horses. Horses have been poisoned by ionophores because of mixing errors in the feed mill, but most mills use separate facilities for their horse and cattle feeds to reduce the likelihood of the problem. If you purchase your feed from a small local mill, ask if they also make feeds for cattle and what safety precautions are taken to guarantee ionophores do not make their way into horse feeds.

Since the potential for moldy corn contamination of feed is so high, do not buy feeds containing corn unless you are assured that the manufacturer routinely screens for fumonisin.

Reject any hay that contains sweet clover. If you aren't sure just by looking at it, ask.

Special care is needed for those horses who share pastures or even barns with other livestock. You must feed horses separately, removing either them or the other animals from the field at feeding time. If horses are removed and cattle or other species fed from bunkers or troughs in the field, make absolutely certain all feed is consumed before you allow the horses access to the field again. Remember, too, that feeds for poultry and other species of birds often contain harmful substances. If feeders are within reach of the horses, they may decide to help themselves.

GIVING YOUR HORSE A PRODUCT DESIGNED
FOR ANOTHER ANIMAL COULD RESULT IN
SERIOUS HEALTH PROBLEMS.

Mineral mixes, blocks or licks formulated for cattle are not appropriate for horses, as mentioned, as they could contain the same potentially harmful substances found in feeds, but in much higher concentration. Horses getting down on their knees to poke their heads through a cattle-level holder is definitely not out of the range of possibility! Plain white salt blocks are safe, as are trace-mineral blocks (the red ones) without added urea (or other nonprotein nitrogen sources) or ionophores. You do need to remember, however, these trace-mineralized are not necessarily formulated to meet the mineral needs of horses — in fact, usually do not — and your horse may need additional mineral supplements as well.

Inside the barn, use separate bins for horse feed and feed for other livestock, and make sure they are clearly labeled. If different people take turns doing the feeding, you may wish to add highly visible (colorful) warnings to tops of bins such as "NOT for horses," "For CATTLE (or Horses, Pigs, etc.) ONLY," etc.

It is a good idea for at least two people to be present when feed is unloaded from bags or the truck into bins. Anyone can make a mistake, but once it is made, it may be irreversible! Always double check the tags on bags or the order slip before unloading into bins. Do not leave bags of feed that are missing their labels around. You may know what they are the day you put them there but not be so sure a week or so later. If a feed doesn't look the same to you or you have any reason to think a mistake may have been made, call the supplier immediately. Spills should be cleaned up promptly, not left in areas where animals may have access to them. (They also attract pesky rodents and other wildlife!)

In real life, there's no need to panic if your horse grabs a mouthful of the steer's dinner when he's walking past. However, getting too-casual an attitude about allowing feeds intended for other species to be given to your horse has a way of leading to too-careless an approach to potentially very serious health problems. Your horse may really love that silage his bovine buddy gets to eat, but resist the temptation to give it to him. Give him carrots instead! PH

13

Essential Electrolytes

*Does the equine equivalent of "Gatorade"
really make a difference
in a horse's performance and health?*

Dissolved in the blood and tissues of the body, electrolytes
are minerals that carry a positive (+) or negative (-) electrical charge. These minerals assist in preserving the correct balance of fluid both inside and outside the cells. They
also function in the generation of nerve impulses, contractions of
muscles, the beating of the heart and processing of wastes — in fact,
electrolytes are involved in virtually every function of the body.

The National Research Council (NRC) estimates the horse requires
a concentration of at least 0.1% of salt (NaCl) in the diet to meet
basic maintenance needs (no work, no pregnancy, no hot weather).
However, few hays and no grains can meet this level. Under conditions of restricted intake, the horse's kidneys can compensate to a
certain extent, secreting less sodium than normal.

Of the other major electrolytes, potassium, calcium, phosphorus
and magnesium can be found in adequate amounts in most common equine diets — at least for horses at maintenance. When you
add exercise, pregnancy or hot weather to the equation, however,
the picture changes.

The efficiency with which the horse can use individual electrolytes in his diet can also be influenced by other factors. For example, the absorption, use and retention/excretion of calcium and
phosphorus is under the control of the hormone parathormone. A
disruption of the balance between calcium and phosphorus can lead
to problems with absorption and the ability to retain one or the other

Horses who sweat profusely, such as endurance horses, experience heavy fluid and electrolyte losses.

of these minerals. (The ratio of calcium to phosphorus in the diet should be about 1.5:1.0 up to 1.8:1.0.)

We know from research with people and animals other than horses that minerals often have a "carrier system" that gets them across the wall of the intestine and into the body via the blood stream. The carrier system is essentially a protein/enzyme that recognizes a part of the mineral in question, latches onto it and causes it to be absorbed. Iron, zinc and copper all compete with each other for absorption in this way.

Magnesium is a critical but often overlooked electrolyte that depends on a carrier system. However, little is known about how it is absorbed or what mechanisms in the body control its blood level. A superficial analysis of common feeds appears to show adequate levels of magnesium. However, magnesium deficiencies — or at least borderline low blood levels — can often be found. Deficiencies can occur in horses even on diets that are relatively "rich" in magnesium, such as those based on alfalfa hay. A closer look at these diets shows they are also very high in calcium.

We know from studies with other animals that calcium and magnesium can share a common carrier system. Assuming this to be the case in the horse, competition for absorption by the high calcium may cause low magnesium levels. Magnesium is also low in most water throughout the United States (certain regions of the Midwest are an exception) — even in mineral-rich hard well water or spring water, not surprisingly, the major mineral is calcium.

Electrolyte losses

Although the horse's body efficiently conserves electrolytes, a certain amount is lost each day through urine, manure, sweat and secretions into the digestive tract. In addition to these normal losses, electrolytes may be lost in large amounts in disease states, such as diarrhea.

Of course, sweating is the avenue of electrolyte loss that most people are familiar with. Sweat tastes salty, and it only makes sense that increased sweating would increase electrolyte losses. However, sweating also increases water loss. **In fact, the water loss is usually more critical than the electrolyte loss, and water should always be replaced first (or at least at the same time).**

Any exercise can cause electrolyte losses. Heavy work that results in even microscopic damage to the muscles makes the walls of the muscle cells "leaky." Because of this, more of the critical intracellular (inside the cell) electrolytes — such as calcium, magnesium and potassium — can be released and cause blood levels to rise above normal after the exercise stops. The kidneys will detect this imbalance and immediately work to correct the situation by causing the excess to be excreted in the urine — all before the cells have a chance to repair themselves and take back in the electrolytes they lost to the blood.

When to supplement electrolytes

Obviously, sodium chloride (salt) should be available free choice as a supplement at all times. Most horses will match their intake of salt to their needs — but not all. In times of hot weather or heavy work, keep a close eye on your horse's salt block. **A horse in heavy work should consume a three-pound salt block (the standard small block you mount on the wall) in approximately two weeks during hot weather or three weeks during cooler weather at the same work load.**

Many people use free-choice salt blocks as their horse's only source of electrolytes year-round without problems. As a general rule, if the horse is not being worked heavily and he makes regular use of his salt block, he may not need additional electrolyte supplementation.

One way to check for dehydration is to lift the horse's upper lip to inspect the color of his gums. They should be a healthy pink.

Supplemental electrolytes should be used only when necessary. For best results, divide the daily dose into several feedings or waterings for horses who will be on the go or exposed to high temperatures (such as trailering on a hot day). For the few horses who need daily supplementation, use the electrolytes on schedule. With horses who need them on a short-term basis (an unusual level of activity or heat exposure), begin supplementation the day before the stressful event and continue for one day past the period of higher demand.

How to give electrolytes

Many horses will readily consume electrolytes mixed in water according to manufacturer's recommendations. This is the preferred route of administration, since the **increased electrolyte needs are always paired with increased water needs. Follow directions carefully.**

It is also important to provide fresh electrolyte-free water and the horse's regular salt block along with the electrolyte-treated water. This means the horse will have his choice of two buckets of water. Providing supplemental electrolytes will also increase the horse's need for plain water, and failure to give it can result in an electrolyte "overload."

To get rid of this overload, the horse will either secrete more water into his intestinal tract or via the kidneys. The result will be a horse who is more dehydrated than before he received electrolytes — exactly what you are trying to avoid.

If you have a horse who will not drink electrolyte-treated water, the electrolytes can be added to the feed or given in paste form. However, be sure the horse has access to an extra bucket of water to allow him to balance out the electrolyte load. **Never allow a horse who receives electrolyte supplements to run out of plain water.**

Electrolyte supplementation guidelines

As a general guideline, consider providing electrolyte supplementation in addition to free-choice salt under the following circumstances:

1. Your horse does not consume adequate salt on his own — a high of one salt block every two weeks for horses in heavy work in hot weather to a low of one salt block every six weeks or so for horses not being worked and in moderate temperature conditions (weather and work will affect normal intake).

2. Your horse has adequate salt intake but shows signs of electrolyte imbalance such as mild dehydration, muscular cramping, tying-up, loss of appetite (a fairly constant early sign of electrolyte imbalance), change in character of manure, weakness, lethargy or decreased urination. However, other potential physical causes must be ruled out by a veterinarian before jumping on low electrolytes as the cause. If the horse checks out as apparently free of any medical problem and has been exercising regularly and/or exercising during hot weather, electrolyte supplementation may indeed be indicated.

3. You know the horse will be asked to work heavily (especially beyond his usual work load), under conditions where feed, water and salt intake will be restricted (or the horse may not eat well) and particularly if the weather is going to be warm enough that the work load will cause him to sweat. Examples of these conditions are a show in hot weather, a packing trip or a heavy load of lessons.

4. The horse has a problem that is known to be influenced by, or causes, electrolyte abnormalities. Prime examples are any muscular problems or diarrhea.

Electrolyte ingredient table

	Sodium Dose	Potassium Dose	Magnesium Dose	Calcium Dose
Summer Games 1 (powder)	6,4884.5 mg (as 16,700 mg NaCl)	3,500 mg	160 mg	170 mg
Ride-Rite (powder)	1,526.5 mg	71 mg	28.4 mg	326.7 mg
Lyte Now 2 (paste)	2,829 mg (as 7,200 mg NaCl)	3,772.8 mg (as 7,200 KCl)	1,326 mg (as 5,200 mg MgC)	1,877 mg (as 5,200 of CaC)
Jug (powder)	8,600 mg	3,100 mg	500 mg	800 mg
Electro-Plex 3 (paste)	625 mg	500 mg		375 mg
Cherry Elite Electrolyte 4 (powder)	15,720 mg (as 40,000 mg NaCl)	6,248 mg	227.2 mg	284 mg
Apple-A-Day (powder)	8,520 mg	3,400 mg	142 mg	1,587 mg

1 Small amounts per dose of phosphorus, copper, iodine, manganese, zinc.

2 Small amounts per dose of copper, iodine, cobalt, manganese, zinc.

3 Potassium, magnesium and calcium are chelated (attached to a protein).

4 Small amounts per dose of lactate, phosphorus, zinc, manganese, iron, copper, cobalt.

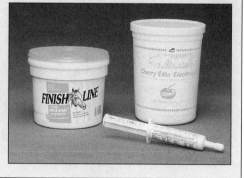

Choosing an electrolyte supplement

Electrolyte supplements come in a wide variety of packages, flavors and consistencies and vary in the types and amounts of electrolytes they contain. We evaluated a cross section. Our comments on these products refer to one dose or serving, as defined by manufacturer's recommendations.

We evaluated flavored electrolyte products and found that, while they smelled appealing as a powder or in solution, there was no appreciable difference in taste to our human tester and no significant improvement in palatability to the horses.

For ease of comparison to other products, remember that the sodium content of NaCl is roughly one-third of the weight (39.3%) — 15 grams of sodium chloride would provide 5.89 grams of sodium.

Bottom line

Choose the electrolyte that meets your horse's needs: For normal, healthy horses, we like Summer Games Electrolyte (Kentucky Equine Research) since it is formulated to match electrolyte losses through sweat, the major route of electrolyte loss in exercising horses or during hot weather. The manufacturer has also taken pains to provide detailed instructions on adjusting the dosage to meet the needs of individual horses, taking the guesswork out of trying to match a particular product to a particular horse.

Note: Equi-Aide, the manufacturer of Jug, also claims this product has been successfully used in a wide variety of conditions with appropriate changes to the dosing schedule.

For short-term electrolyte supplementation for the horse in light or moderate work, choose from Jug, Lyte Now (Pro Formula) or Apple-A-Day (Finish Line) to get the job done.

For horses who don't take adequate salt on their own, Cherry Elite Electrolyte (Farnam) might be just the thing. It contains about twice as much salt as you would normally need. Check with your veterinarian first, and provide constant access to plain water when using this product, unless instructed to do otherwise by your veterinarian.

For horses with a history of muscle problems or doing short duration bouts of high-intensity work, we especially like Lyte Now. The extra calcium, magnesium and potassium in this product make it uniquely suited to cover the likelihood of losses of intracellular electrolytes arising from over-stressed muscles.

For endurance horses, or any horse that must work for prolonged periods throughout the day (trail riding, lessons and so forth), Ride-Rite (Advanced Biological Concepts) is tailor-made. It represents the closest match to recommendations published for oral replacement fluids for endurance horses.

Endurance horses with a history of thumps (proven by blood tests to be associated with a low calcium level) would probably do best on the extra calcium provided by Apple-A-Day. Check with the veterinarian who knows the horse's blood test results for advice on how much to use and in what concentration.

Electro-Plex (Oral-X Corp.) is a paste formulated to match the composition found in amino-acid intravenous solutions. As the chart shows, this product contains only 625 mg of sodium chloride. Since a horse's sodium requirements are estimated to be as much as six grams higher than maintenance, even for light work, this product will not make much of a dent in the horse's needs. However, it might provide a stimulus for the horse to drink and, hopefully, take in more salt on his own.

Also note that while some manufacturers recommend withholding regular water in an attempt to have the horse be forced to drink the electrolyte water, it is more important that the horse take in adequate water than that he drink the electrolyte solution.

Electrolytes

SODIUM AND CHLORIDE: *NaCl, common table salt, is the major electrolyte of the body. Salt is composed of two electrolyte ions (charged particles) — sodium (Na+) and chloride (Cl-). It is found in much higher concentration outside the cells (in the blood and other fluids surrounding the cells) than in the cells themselves.*

The "saltiness" of blood is measured as it is filtered through the kidneys. This way, the body knows how much water to release in the urine to keep the concentration of salt in the blood at its normal level.

When the horse becomes dehydrated and the blood sodium level is more concentrated, sweating will slow or even stop as the body attempts to preserve the critical balance of salt to water. However, without adequate sweating, dangerous overheating can result.

POTASSIUM: *Inside the cells, potassium (K+) assumes the role as the major positive-charged electrolyte. One of potassium's major roles is to keep the sensitivity of nerves and muscles at a normal level — not under- or over-reactive to impulses telling them to contract. This includes both the skeletal muscles and the heart muscle.*

Even relatively small changes in total potassium (potassium inside and outside cells) can negatively affect athletic performance. Because the sensitivity of the nerves and muscles is based upon maintaining a fairly constant gradient (difference) between the potassium and sodium inside the cells compared to the potassium and sodium outside the cells, the body works hard to keep the blood's potassium level within a narrow normal range. To do this the blood sometimes "robs" potassium from the inside of cells.

Consequently, a blood test is not always a reliable method of picking up problems with potassium, because it only indicates the amount of potassium circulating in the blood. It doesn't tell about potassium within the cells. But, if blood levels are low, you can be sure the level inside the cells is in even worse shape.

CALCIUM: *When we hear calcium, we think of bones and teeth. This is indeed a major function of calcium in the body, and most of the calcium is found within bones and teeth. However, calcium in its ionic form (Ca++) is also an important electrolyte. Like potassium and magnesium, it is critical to the normal function of muscles and nerve tissue. Also like potassium, the levels of calcium in the blood are closely regulated by the body to be kept in a narrow normal range. If need be, the body again will rob itself — the bones and the other body cells — to maintain its calcium blood level.*

MAGNESIUM: *Magnesium is probably the most overlooked electrolyte. Although found in much smaller amounts than many other electrolytes, it has critical roles to play. Magnesium functions as a "co-factor" in over 300 enzyme reactions within the body. This means if magnesium is not present, or is present in an insufficient amount, each of the 300 reactions will suffer.*

Magnesium is the critical co-factor for reactions that involve the burning of glucose in the presence of oxygen — the most important power source for all aerobic (oxygen-using) exercise. Magnesium is involved in the metabolism of fats and proteins, as well. It is also essential for DNA to be able to send messages to the cells. Magnesium is an essential link in the chain of command from the "brain" of the cell — its nucleus — to the other structures within a cell. Magnesium is required for normal muscle function, especially for relaxation of a muscle.

PHOSPHORUS: *Phosphorus is also involved in formation of bone. About 85 percent of the body's phosphorus is located inside the bones in a solid form. The remainder is distributed between the blood and the interior of the cells. Inside cells, phosphorus is absolutely essential to the normal metabolism of carbohydrates, fats and proteins, as well as the generation and storage of energy from these basic fuels.*

MANGANESE: *Like magnesium, manganese is present in relatively tiny amounts compared to many other electrolytes, but it is essential to the formation of normal connective tissues (the tissues that hold the body together — i.e., the "gristle" in the meat you eat) and the formation of normal joint cartilage. Manganese also plays a role in the metabolism of fat and the creation of DNA.*

COPPER: *Copper is present in basically tiny amounts compared to the "major electrolytes." But, the utilization of iron to make healthy red blood cells requires copper. Formation of the protective outer coatings (sheaths) on nerves also requires copper, as does the production of skin pigment and the formation of healthy collagen (connective tissue) — the major component of tendons and ligaments. Similarly, healthy joint cartilage can only be produced when there is a proper amount of copper.* PH

For contact information on specific products mentioned, please see page 204.

14

Finding The Right
Vitamin B Supplement

We all know B vitamins are important.
But should you supplement your horse's diet with
additional B vitamins or not? How much will you
need? And, how do you choose the right product?

As a general rule, a healthy horse at rest or even in light/occasional work, with access to pasture and a high-quality diet, will more than likely do quite well without B-vitamin supplementation. However, even horses in these circumstances may develop problems of the type that could signal that B vitamins are not at optimal levels — most notably, problems with skin, coat or hoof quality. If you are going to supplement as an insurance policy (similar to people taking their One-A-Days), the levels found in most high-quality general vitamin supplements should work just fine.

But, not all horses have perfectly performing bodies or live a life of leisure. For those horses, vitamin-B supplementation may be a real need, not just a casual option.

For years it was thought that horses didn't need B-vitamin supplementation. But, since then we've learned that many things can influence how well the horse can supply himself with B vitamins, and ideas are changing about if and when B vitamins should be given.

B vitamins are naturally found in grains and brans; but hays, grasses and other roughages, such as beet pulp, are relatively poor sources. Since many horses are on pasture/hay only or limited grain diets, we know it's likely they are not taking in sufficient amounts.

The B vitamins inside the horse's intestines will not do him any good unless they are absorbed into the bloodstream. We don't know how efficient this process is. Most of the absorption probably takes place in the first portions of the intestinal tract — the small intestine. If levels do not begin to rise until farther along, it is questionable how much good they do the horse.

Fortunately, most horses are not likely to develop full-blown deficiencies because, while they are unable to manufacture B vitamins themselves, the micro-organisms (bacterium) inside their intestinal tract operate like B-vitamin factories, which is why it pays to keep those little bugs healthy.

Anything that interferes with normal digestion, such as heavy parasite burdens or scarring of the intestines, may also negatively impact the absorption of B vitamins. And, if the food material moves along the intestine faster than normal (such as with diarrhea), the B vitamins are less available for absorption.

Stress and the B vitamins

In times of stress, whether emotional/psychological (training, competition with other horses in the field) or physical (injury, infection, heavy exercise, shipping, pregnancy, growth, environmental toxins or drugs), the body's systems are all taxed. The heart beats faster, and energy is turned out quicker, which increases the need for all nutrients, including vitamins.

A horse at work will require significantly more B vitamins than a horse at pasture.

Without proper nutrition, stress quickly takes its toll in terms of immunity and nervous system health. **"Stressed-out" horses, like stressed-out people, are more likely to get sick, become jumpy, irritable, off feed and just plain out of sorts.**

Supplementing the B group during stress is especially important, because the horse's body cannot store these vitamins. What the horse cannot use will be eliminated, usually within 24 hours. This is why, if you are feeding B vitamins, they must be provided on a regular, daily basis.

B vitamins and appetite

Is your horse a picky eater? B-vitamin supplements may stimulate his appetite. And, as an added bonus, he may become more alert and eager. Did he lack B vitamins? You may never know, but if he responds — who cares? It's a "chicken or egg" situation. He could have been sluggish and eating poorly because he needed more B vitamins. Or because he wasn't eating correctly, he needed more B vitamins, and sluggishness was the result of inadequate nutrition.

Bs for maintenance/insurance

If you have decided your horse could benefit from B-vitamin supplementation for "insurance" or specific health problems, your best place to search is in multivitamin/mineral products. Be sure to take into account the type of hay as well as what is contained in any other supplements, complete feed or fortified grains that you are feeding.

Since these "multi" supplements also supply other vitamins and minerals, it is important to choose one that will meet your horse's other nutritional needs. Of particular concern is the major minerals calcium and phosphorus. **Supplements containing high calcium and/or high ratios of calcium to phosphorus should not be fed to horses receiving alfalfa hay, as alfalfa is already imbalanced (high calcium, low phosphorus) in this respect.**

Very high vitamin A levels (in the order of 30,000 to 40,000 IU/day) are also potentially toxic to horses receiving high-quality alfalfa, which is an excellent source of vitamin A.

Reasonable minimums would be:
- Thiamine 25 to 50 mg/day
- Riboflavin 10 to 20 mg/day*
- Niacin 25 to 50 mg/day*
- Pantothenic acid 10 to 20 mg/day*
- Pyridoxine 2 to 10 mg/day*
- Biotin 2 mg/day,
- Folic acid 1 mg/day.

Values marked with * are those for which solid equine-specific recommendations do not exist; numbers are extrapolated from what is known in other species. The above are all conservative dosages. Pregnancy, growth, exercise and specific health problems can require much higher dosages.

B vitamins and blood counts

Several B vitamins play important roles in the manufacture of red blood cells and, for this reason, are always a major ingredient in "blood builders" and tonics. Supplementing B vitamins often leads to slight increases in the number of red blood cells. Veterinarians are not sure if these small increases make any difference in the horse's health or performance, or even if they are actually the result of the horse making more red blood cells. It may just be that his metabolism is functioning more efficiently, and this signals the body to send more oxygen to the cells by releasing more red blood cells from their storage site in the horse's spleen. In any event, B vitamins should always be on the treatment list for horses with low red blood cell counts.

Maintenance B products

There are countless multivitamin/mineral supplements that may be suitable for the "insurance" type B supplementation. We've chosen a few that are typical, listed in our Chart I on page 114. While they show some variation in levels of specific vitamins, most will meet or exceed your horse's needs for all B vitamins.

Our first choice in this category is **Equine Supplement** (Vita-Key). Because it does not contain calcium or phosphorus, it is appropriate to use with any type of hay. This product contains generous, but not excessive, amounts of all the most important B vitamins (it also has good trace mineral and antioxidant vitamin levels to complete the picture).

If you are looking only to boost the Bs, you might consider using **Ultra Fire** (Finish Line) at half the recommended dosage. This would give you levels of B vitamins in line with maintenance-type products, and at considerably lower cost.

B vitamin requirements

Vitamin	NRC Recommended Level for Horses	Equine Equivalent of Human Dose
B1 (Thiamine)	3 mg/kg of diet for maintenance, reproduction and growth.	7.5 mg/day sedentary 250-1000 mg/day exercising 5 mg/kg of diet for exercise
B2 (Riboflavin)	2 mg/kg of diet	8.5 mg/day sedentary 125-1000 mg/day exercising
B3 (Niacin)	No recommendation	13.2 mg/day sedentary 180 - 600 mg/day exercising
B5 (Pantothenic Acid)	No recommendation	10 mg/day sedentary 20 - 200 mg/day exercising
B6 (Pyridoxine)	No recommendation	2 mg/day 10 - 50 mg/day exercising
B12 (Cyanocobalamin)	No recommendation	3 - 8 mcg/day sedentary None above sedentary needs
Biotin	2 mg/day	180 - 600 mcg/day sedentary 300 - 5000 mcg/day exercising
Folic Acid	No recommendation	200 mcg/day sedentary 800 - 4800 mcg/day exercising

High-potency Bs

While the need for B vitamins increases for horses in circumstances such as performance, infection, nonspecific stress, history of gastrointestinal problems and so forth, the horse's need for major minerals does not. **It is therefore both unsafe and wasteful to try to meet the horse's needs for increased Bs by increasing the dosage of a general multivitamin/mineral supplement.**

To locate a high-potency B supplement, check among the products designed for performance enhancement or listed as blood builders. They can supply the increased B-vitamin needs without adding other potentially toxic vitamins or major minerals, and they are usually compatible with multivitamin and mineral supplements you might already be feeding.

The major concern with products in these categories is their iron level. People are conditioned to associate iron with good blood counts, because iron is often deficient in human diets. However, this is not the case with horses, and **overfeeding iron can be toxic. We recommend going with the lowest iron level you can find (preferably at or below 50 mg).**

Many of these supplements will also contain added trace minerals. Since needs for trace minerals can also increase during many of these conditions (i.e., pregnancy and conditions with high production of free radicals, such as heavy exercise or infections), this is a plus. But, to avoid disrupting the ratio of trace minerals in an already balanced diet, look for a formula that contains zinc and magnesium in equivalent amounts and at levels approximately three times higher than copper.

Frequently asked questions about B-vitamin supplementation

Question: Is more better, or like calcium and phosphorus, is the balance important? Should I just go for the most Bs at the lowest cost?

Answer: The B vitamins work in concert; that is, to properly perform their jobs of energy generation, normal nervous system function, red-cell production and so forth, the B vitamins must be supplemented as a group.

The best starting point is to supplement Bs at their recommended minimal daily level, especially if the horse is not receiving any grain or other good natural source of Bs. When specific numbers are not known for horses, manufacturers will usually use the human requirement adjusted upward by a factor of six for the horse.

More is not necessarily better. For example, high doses of

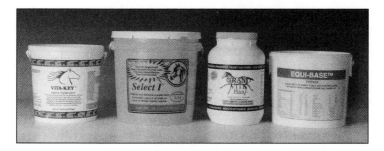

*thiamine can have a depressant effect in some horses (at
a range of 500 to 1,000 mg/day). Niacin can have the
opposite effect, causing agitation that may be related to
the high-dosage side effects of skin burning and tingling.*

*Long-term use of high dosages of B6 in people has caused
altered sensations in the limbs. High doses of the Bs
involved in energy generation from carbohydrates, such as
niacin, may block the use of fats as a fuel and make energy
generation less efficient at aerobic work loads. Higher
doses of one or another of the B vitamins may be indicated
with specific problems but should always be given in conjunction with minimal requirements of the other Bs.*

**Q: Labels can be confusing. One is high in one thing,
another high in something else. Is there a priority
order, beyond just the B that you are concerned about,
such as thiamine for the nervous horse?**

*A: Of greatest concern are the Bs that research has
identified as sometimes being deficient in horses (thiamine and folic acid) and those that intestinal studies
show are in short supply in the small intestine (thiamine,
pyridoxine, biotin, folic acid). Horses with specific needs
for increased levels of Bs, such as in exercise, stress,
pregnancy, etc., also may require more than they can get
from diet and intestinal manufacture alone. One B that
you probably do not have to worry about is B12.*

**Q: Does it matter if I'm feeding a fortified grain mix or
a complete feed? Can I overdo this B thing?**

*A: As mentioned above, it is possible to overdo it with
some of the B vitamins. However, fortified grains and*

B Vitamin Levels in "Multi" Supplements — Chart I

	Grand Vite (Grand Meadows)	Equi-Base (Uckele)	Select I or Select II (Select The Best)	Vita-Key Equine Supplement (Vita-Key)	Accel (Vita-Flex)
B1	26	12.5	2.5	100	14
B2	25	10.9	16.6	30	62.5
Niacin	62.5	49.3	41.6	125	31.25
B5	24	21.4	30	9	12.5
B6	11	6.25	3.33	15	15.19
B12	75 mcg	43.8 mcg	66 mcg	200 mcg	138 mcg
Biotin	2.5	0.8	1.66	1.66	0.5
Folic Acid	30	10	11.6	12	5
Serving Size	2 oz	5 oz	3 oz	2 oz	2 oz
Cost per oz.	$0.31	$0.08	$0.21	$0.35	$0.22
Cost per dose	$0.62	$0.40	$0.63	$0.70	$0.44
Best w/ type of hay	Alfalfa	Grass	I – Alfalfa II – Grass	either	Grass

(Amounts in mg/oz unless otherwise noted)

B Vitamin Levels in High-Potency Supplements — Chart II

	Ultra Fire (Finish Line)	Iron Horse (Finish Line)	MaxPlus (Vita-Flex)	Horse Honey 2X (Uckele)
Per oz				
B1	260	75	30	100
B2	260	75	24	30
Niacin	580	160	210	100
B5	263.6	160	42	250
B6	80	22	6	10
B12	164	100	100	125
Biotin	2.5	0	0	0
Folic Acid	7.9	10	6	10
Iron	2.27	300	50	300
Serving size	0.5 oz	2 oz	2 oz	2 oz
Cost per oz.	$1.06	$0.50	$1.08	$0.81
Cost per dose	$0.53	$1.00	$2.16	$1.62

(Amounts in mg/oz unless otherwise noted)

complete feeds usually do not contain large amounts of supplemental B vitamins. The "complete" in complete feed only means it contains enough fiber for normal digestion. These feeds may actually contain lower levels of B vitamins than straight grain. The fact that a B vitamin is listed on the ingredient list does not mean much. You have to go to the part of the label that says "guaranteed analysis." Unless the vitamin is on that list, it is probably either present in amounts too small to be worth mentioning or the level in the feed could vary from bag to bag (and you cannot depend on it).

Q: What about Brewer's yeast? We hear it recommended for people — is that a good/cheap source of B vitamins?

A: *Brewer's yeast does contain a wide array of B vitamins. However, they are present in fairly low concentrations. To get the same level of supplementation as is found in most multivitamin/mineral products, you would have to feed half a pound or more of the Brewer's yeast. Not many horses will eat that much, and the amount fed negates any cost advantage. You may hear claims that Brewer's yeast is better because it is a natural source. However, there is no evidence that natural sources are absorbed better or work better than manufactured vitamins.*

Q: Is there any reason you couldn't give your horse human vitamins or something from the health-food store?

> *A: There is no particular reason you could not use B vitamins from the health-food store for your horse, but the formulation in multiple-B supplements may not be appropriate for horses. For example, horses appear to need more thiamine and biotin than would be predicted just by adjusting the human minimal daily requirements for the horse's size. Human vitamins are also usually more expensive to feed.*

High-potency B products

Chart II on page 114 lists four representative high-potency B or "blood builder" products. **Ultra Fire** is a powder; all the rest are liquids.

Our overwhelming choice in this category is **Ultra Fire**. It is extremely potent and contains almost no iron. It was also the only product that contained any biotin (although a horse with a specific need for biotin should be placed on a biotin supplement at higher doses). The price is definitely the best, as well.

We also found it to be highly palatable. For the horse who is not eating well, you can mix the powder with a small amount of corn syrup to make a sticky paste and deposit this on the back of the horse's tongue, or use a small amount of water and a syringe to squirt it into the back of the horse's mouth. █PH█

For contact information on specific products mentioned, please see page 204.

15

The Value Of Antioxidants

*What do rusty cars, brown apples and
your horse have in common?
They are all casualties in the oxidation wars.*

If you could feed your horse something that not only maximizes the good and necessary metabolic functions but also waits in the ranks to neutralize toxic waste, would you do it? Of course you would. You'd help him win the toxic-waste war with antioxidants.

Every minute of every day your horse's cellular "engines" are performing vital functions, such as burning foods for energy (generating horsepower!), neutralizing toxins and fighting infections. Unfortunately, these good activities also generate toxic waste that results, over time, in aging, weakening of tissues, loss of memory and other brain changes, damage to genetic material and even cancer and heart disease. Once done, the damage is irreversible. But, the good news is we can help the horse fight toxic waste and slow this process.

Antioxidants are substances that counteract harmful byproducts of oxidation reactions. An oxidation reaction is what happens when your car rusts or oxidizes. The metal is eaten up, and the byproduct, rust, takes its place. So, how does this happen?

If you remember back to chemistry class, oxygen in its gaseous form (free in the air around us or dissolved in blood) has no electrical charge. However, when oxygen or an oxygen-containing compound is involved in a chemical reaction, it loses one of its electrons, becomes imbalanced, electrically charged and is then called a "free radical." **Free radicals are unstable and actively seek their original electrically neutral state by reacting with other substances nearby.**

Inside the body, oxidation reactions occur constantly, producing free radicals every time the body burns an energy source — carbohydrate, fat or protein. **Free-radical production is related to how much energy is generated. Therefore, exercise increases the number of free radicals.**

Free radicals are also generated when the body must metabolize (break down) a drug or a toxin from the environment or when fighting infections. The body is bombarded by microorganisms every minute of every day. It is challenged every time even a small number of organisms make their way past the normal barriers of intact skin or mucus membranes (lining the nose, mouth, lungs, digestive tract, urinary tract and reproductive tract).

The battle begins

It's a war, and the bad guys (free radicals) are always on the prowl. **Free radicals are unstable compounds and, in their electrically charged state, they "attack" tissues around them, looking to steal an electron to neutralize their charge.** Left unchecked, they do as much damage to the inside of a body as they do to the outside of your car.

The mucus-membrane surfaces, the walls of cells throughout the body, the internal structures of cells such as the mitochondria ("furnaces" where foods are burned), and even DNA, the genetic material, are all at risk of damage from free radicals.

Fortunately, the body is equipped with an assortment of mechanisms for capturing and neutralizing free radicals. These include enzymes such as superoxide dismutase, glutathione peroxidase and catalase — all fancy, scientific names for enzymes that can neutralize free radicals. Uric acid and essential fatty acids can help, too. The most attention has been focused recently on antioxidant vitamins.

Vitamin C

Every cook knows the way to prevent fruit from browning is to coat it with ascorbic acid. Ascorbic acid is vitamin C, one of the most important vitamins in fighting against oxidation. It is present in large amounts in citrus fruits and to some extent in other vegetables and plants, including grasses.

One of the water-soluble vitamins, vitamin C is present in the body in the body fluids and is not stored in fat or body organs. Any vitamin C not used in the course of a day is excreted in urine.

Vitamin C is capable on its own of neutralizing free radicals. We see this when cut apples are "protected" by being sprinkled with lemon juice. **Vitamin C is the major antioxidant found in the fluids coating the inside of the lung.** It protects lung tissues from free radicals generated when the immune system is fighting infections and from toxic and irritating chemicals that may be breathed in.

Vitamin C has been found to be low in people with asthma and reactive-airway disease (the equivalent of "heaves" in horses).

Vitamin C is also the major protecting antioxidant for capillaries, the tiniest of the arteries. Substances called bioflavinoids, also present in large concentration in citrus fruits, assist vitamin C in these functions.

Vitamin C also functions by "regenerating" other antioxidant substances. For example, when vitamin E has been used to neutralize a free radical, it is no longer effective. Vitamin C can transfer the free radical from vitamin E onto itself, returning vitamin E to an active form. There is some experimental evidence that vitamin C can have this rejuvenating effect on other antioxidants as well.

The National Research Council (NRC) gives no recommended dietary intake of vitamin C for horses, because horses do not develop a disease due to vitamin C deficiency. However, nutritionists who have looked at vitamin C and the horse know that stress, infection,

The harder a horse works, the more free radicals he produces, and the greater his need for antioxidant supplementation.

injury, work and winter weather can drop vitamin C levels in the blood to virtually zero. The horse therefore needs a constant supply of vitamin C either from manufactured vitamin C or from the diet.

There are not enough good studies available in horses to say you should definitely give you horse vitamin C supplements. However, based on work in other species (including animals, which, like the horse, can manufacture vitamin C), vitamin C supplementation can be beneficial under the following circumstances:

- growth
- injury (including burns, muscle injury, tendon injury)
- heavy exercise
- muscle problems such as tying-up
- breathing difficulty
- infections
- lung bleeding
- prevention of infections
- decreasing symptoms of viral infection and speeding resolution of infections.

It takes a minimum of 4.5 grams of vitamin C per day to create any change in the horse's blood level of vitamin C. A daily intake of about six to seven grams would be needed to provide a "pharmacologically active" dose of vitamin C.

Vitamin A

Vitamin A is the vitamin that imparts yellow or orange color to fresh fruits and vegetables. It is present in high amounts in carrots, sweet potatoes, cantaloupes and apricots, as well as such green vegetables as broccoli and spinach. Vitamin A is also present in fresh pastures and in hays, with alfalfa being the best source. However, vitamin A activity is lost with storage. Naturally occurring vitamin A exists in the form of carotenoids, pigments that the body converts to vitamin A. The most well known is beta-carotene.

As an antioxidant, vitamin A's most important role is in the prevention of cholesterol breakdown into harmful forms, which result in heart disease, at least in people and some other animals, and in protecting the lungs and probably the skin and mucus membranes of the digestive tract from toxins than can cause cancer. Vitamin A's antioxidant role is much less important in horses than in people, since horses are not prone to developing heart disease of this type (i.e., "clogged arteries") and do not have the same level of exposure to carcinogens as most people.

Vitamin A's other functions include maintaining healthy skin, preserving and enhancing vision, especially night vision, and in the normal production of sperm and ova (eggs).

Because vitamin A is fat-soluble and stored in the body fat and in the liver, supplying an excess can result in toxicity. Damage from toxicity of vitamin A includes the formation of calcified plaques in the skin and abnormalities of the bones.

A horse on lush green pasture or being fed good-quality alfalfa hay needs no vitamin A supplementation — in fact, it should be avoided. Horses on poor-quality grass hays may need extra A in the winter. To be on the safe side, it is probably better to give the horse up to one pound of carrots per day than to fool around with vitamin A supplements. About the only time vitamin A supplements would be recommended would be for broodmares in the late winter and early spring months. Research indicates short-term supplementation of mares may improve their fertility, particularly if early season breeding is desired.

Feeding your horse carrots is a safe way to be sure his vitamin A needs are met while avoiding toxicity.

Vitamin E

In many ways, vitamin E is the king of antioxidant vitamins in the horse. As an antioxidant, vitamin E protects body cells and all structures within the cells from free-radical damage. It is most important to those cells — such as muscle cells and cells of the immune system — where free-radical generation is common.

The richest natural sources of vitamin E are vegetable oils. However, processing destroys large amounts of this vitamin, and you must use "natural cold-pressed" oils to get maximal benefit. Pastures and high-quality hays, as well as grains, also supply some vitamin E. As you might guess, since vitamin E is found in oils, vitamin

E is a fat-soluble vitamin stored in body fat. However, levels drop off quickly when vitamin E-deficient diets are fed (studies document vitamin E levels drop during winter when no fresh pasture is available). Also, even though it is stored to some extent, vitamin E appears to have low toxicity even at high levels.

Most horse owners have heard about vitamin E benefiting horses with tying-up syndrome. Vitamin E has been shown to increase the activity of an enzyme called glutathione reductase. Without normal functioning of this enzyme and adequate levels of vitamin E, the free radicals generated during exercise of any kind would damage the muscle cells and the important energy-generating equipment inside them.

Damaged cells do not function normally. Enzymes and critical electrolytes leak out into the blood, and the result is anything from mild cramping and soreness to full-blown tying up. **Vitamin E cannot prevent all cases of tying up. However, it is well documented to at least assist in controlling this problem and in preventing severe muscle damage.**

No one really knows exactly how much vitamin E the horse needs, let alone how much should be provided for maximal health/performance and/or for treatment of muscle problems. Estimates for daily requirements for horses at maintenance (doing no work) may be as low as 600 to 1,800 IU per day. However, the NRC estimates that levels as high as 10,000 units per day for a 1,100-pound horse are still safe, and these high levels are often recommended for horses with muscle problems or horses in heavy work.

Selenium

Selenium assists vitamin E in all its antioxidant properties. **Studies in horses have clearly shown that selenium supplementation can increase a horse's response to vaccinations (better protection). This occurs both when vitamin E and selenium are used together and when selenium is used alone.**

In addition to this improved immune function, selenium assists in the protection of muscle cells and muscle-cell internal structures from free-radical damage, again, working in concert with vitamin E. As with all the well-studied antioxidants, selenium is protective against toxins and irritants.

Although selenium is clearly a beneficial element, it can be toxic. The official NRC safe level is up to one ppm of the diet (one mg of selenium for each kg of hay/grain). However, this is being

Guidelines for antioxidant supplementation

Problem	Appropriate Supplementation
Muscle pain	Vitamin E, beginning at 2,000 IU/day — up to 10,000 IU/day.
Tying up	Selenium up to 5 ppm in total diet — toxic when over 5 ppm. Generally safe at up to 2 mg/day unless high selenium soil levels.
Breathing problems	Vitamin C, minimum 4.5 grams/day; Bioflavinoids/hesperidin, 10 to 20 grams/day; Can also try grape-seed extract at 500 to 1,000 mg/day.
Frequent Infections	Vitamin C, 5.0 to 10.0 grams/day; Trace minerals copper, zinc, manganese.
Stress*	Vitamin C, 4.5 grams/day; Bioflavinoids, 10 mg/day; Trace minerals copper, zinc and manganese; Vitamin E, 2,000 IU/ day.
Heavy air or industrial pollution	Vitamin A, 30,000 IU/day — toxic at higher amounts; Vitamin C, 7.0 grams/day; Bioflavinoids, 20 grams/day; Grape-seed extract, 1,000 mg/day.

*Stress — includes shipping, infection, wound, pre- and postsurgery, heavy exercise, weaning, change of environment.

re-evaluated, and many nutritionists believe that number is too low. Unfortunately, levels in the soils and, therefore levels in the diet, vary greatly across the United States. Some portions of the country are low, while others have extremely high selenium content. Before considering a selenium supplement, consult your local agricultural extension agent and/or your veterinarian for guidelines.

Copper, zinc, chromium, manganese, magnesium

Several other minerals have been clearly identified as having antioxidant properties, thus protecting the cells from direct damage and guarding against toxins and cancer-producing substances. These minerals are active either on their own (where they are termed "scavengers," roaming around gobbling up stray free radicals) or as critical cofactors to major antioxidant-enzyme systems such as glutathione reductase or superoxide dismutase.

Once again, we find that tissues with a normally high level of free-radical generation (muscle and the immune system cells) benefit the most from appropriate levels of these key minerals. ▣

16

Supplements For Hooves

If you think that feeding for healthy hooves
is simply a matter of sprinkling gold dust
on your horse's feed, think again.
We'll help you make sense of a complicated subject.

Our study of feed supplements for healthy hooves indicates that compositions of hoof supplements, as well as opinions of nutritionists, vary widely regarding appropriate supplements and dosages.

Biotin is one of the family of B vitamins and has many important functions involving fats, carbohydrates and proteins. Of greatest significance to the health of hooves is its function in protein metabolism. Hooves (like hair and our own nails) are very high in protein. **Deficiency of biotin appears classically as dry, scaly skin and poor hoof quality.**

Biotin is present in large amounts in soybean meal and oats. Hays, corn, barley and pasture grasses are all either low in biotin or contain biotin that may not be "bioavailable" (i.e., in a form that the horse can absorb and use).

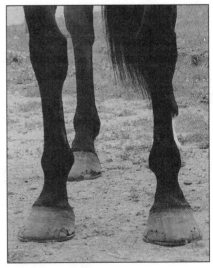

Broken, shelly feet can be the result of shoeing neglect or poor/inadequate nutrition.

In addition to dietary sources, biotin can be found in the intestinal tract of the horse, being made by micro-organisms in the intestine. It shows up in any significant amounts only inside the large intestine, where its ability to be absorbed is highly debatable.

For general health maintenance, it is estimated by the National Research Council that horses require a minimum of 2 mg per day of biotin. **Clinical reports indicating that adding 10 to 30 mg of biotin per day to the diet of the horse has a beneficial effect on hooves began to appear in the early 1990s — and biotin supplements soon followed.**

TO AVOID HOOF-HEALTH PROBLEMS,

BEGIN WITH A PROPER BASIC DIET.

One difficulty in documenting the effects of biotin supplementation is that results vary from horse to horse. Also, it takes approximately nine months for the quality of the hoof to begin to improve. Most recently, sophisticated research has shed some light on the biotin question by using electron microscopes to take pictures of various layers of the hoof and internal structures of the hoof (at magnifications of several thousand times). Deficiency of biotin appears to be related to characteristic abnormalities in the outer layer of the hoof, causing the creation of microscopic vacuoles (holes). These weaken the outer wall, resulting in splitting, cracking and excessive dryness.

Biotin supplementation

Advocates of biotin supplementation point to a low biotin level in feed, the likelihood of poor availability of biotin in the intestine and a number of clinical reports verifying its effectiveness.

Equally strong opponents argue that biotin is only required in very small amounts and is available both from the diet and the intestinal tract. Perhaps most *convincing for this side is that **research involving large numbers of horses shows that horses responding completely to biotin alone probably constitute less than five percent of all horses with hoof problems.** They can be identified by characteristic changes in the outer hoof wall seen only under an electron microscope (not a viable diagnostic tool for the average horse owner!) and by checking blood levels of biotin (potentially more feasible but will probably cost as much as a several-month supply of hoof supplement).*

Methionine

Methionine is an amino acid, a specific building block of protein. Methionine is known to be essential for virtually every other animal species, so most nutritionists assume, understandably, that it also has to be supplied to the horse. Unfortunately, methionine is in short supply in most plain grains and hays, with high protein meals such as soybean and non-vegetable protein supplements (milk products) being better sources. A major protein in the hoof wall is cystine, an amino acid that the horse obtains either from the diet or by conversion of methionine. Cystine comes from the same sources as methionine, but often in lower amounts. Fortunately, the horse can convert methionine into cystine with relative ease as it is needed.

Both cystine and methionine are sulfur-containing amino acids. It is a special interconnection of the sulfur atoms between the proteins that forms the hoof wall and gives it its strength.

Normal dietary methionine may be inadequate to meet minimal needs under the following circumstances: during periods of rapid growth, when methionine is being used up at increased rates (wound healing, etc.) or when absorption is being negatively affected by virtually any problem with the intestinal tract.

Zinc

The third nutrient found to be linked directly to healthy hooves is zinc, a mineral that serves as an essential cofactor in an estimated 100 or more enzymatic reactions in the body. **Supplementation with zinc has been shown to be effective in improving various abnormalities of the hoof.**

The precise requirement for zinc in the horse's diet is not clearly known, but the best estimate (by the National Research Council) seems to be around 40 to 50 ppm (mg of zinc for each kilogram of hay/grain consumed). **This works out to a daily requirement of about 200 to 240 mg of zinc for an average horse in light work.**

Only timothy hay easily meets this, with levels from 38 to 55 ppm. Other grass hays (i.e., orchard grass, 36 to 40 ppm) come close, but alfalfa hay ranges from 16.2 to 24 ppm (values depend upon stage of hay when cut). Soybean meal is a good source (50 ppm and up), and dehydrated cane molasses are fairly good (31 ppm), but oats (6 ppm) and corn (19 ppm) are low.

Ionic or chelated zinc?

The chemical form of zinc may influence absorption. Studies in other species clearly show zinc in ionic form (mineral salt) is much less available than zinc combined with an amino acid (chelated). Chelation increases absorption of all minerals also — not just zinc. The bioavailability (that critical word again!) of zinc methionine is 3.38 times greater than that of zinc oxide in other species and approximately twice as great as zinc sulfate. This is probably true for the horse as well, but how much of an advantage the chelated form is for the horse has not been determined. As you would expect, the requirement for zinc is increased by growth, pregnancy, disease, injury and even heavy athletic activity.

Other nutrients

An added factor arises when an approach to the health of the entire foot, not just the outer hoof wall, is adopted. The quality of the frog, soles and tissues underlying the outer hoof wall are all influenced by nutritional factors other than the basic three nutrients (zinc, methionine and biotin) identified to date as important to hoof health. **The horse needs adequate total levels of protein in his diet (not just methionine and cystine), as well as vitamin C and copper to keep the foot (not to mention all connective tissues such as tendons and joints) healthy.**

Copper is a mineral well recognized to be essential to the formation of normal connective tissue, but the amount required is also a point of great controversy among nutritionists. Estimates range from 10 ppm for adult horses at maintenance to as high as 40 ppm for pregnant and growing horses. Athletes probably need more than inactive horses. Copper status is further complicated by the fact that other minerals (such as zinc and iron) can compete for absorption or block copper's activity.

Overall diet

How much of each nutrient a supplement should contain will depend on the horse's overall condition and the diet you are feeding.

If the horse has foot problems beyond dryness and a tendency for the hoof to split at ground surface, it is reasonable to use a supplement that promotes the overall health of connective tissues. We are speaking of problems such as quarter cracks, a history of abscesses, an abnormal coronary band, "tender feet," thrush, nails ripping out and shoes coming off. Here, attention to total dietary protein, calcium-and-phosphorus balance, zinc-to-copper ratio, copper levels and supplemental vitamin C is important, but opinions differ.

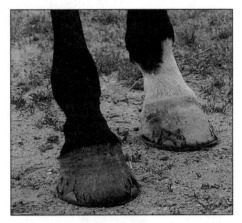

Once dietary imbalances have been corrected, it takes approximately nine months for the quality of the hoof to improve substantially.

Evaluation of supplements

We looked at a variety of hoof supplements. Their ingredients are summarized in the chart later in this chapter. Needs will vary depending upon the hoof problems encountered and the diet fed. (Note: **Winner's Daily** (Pro Formula) is not sold specifically as a hoof supplement. However, it is a good overall supplement and was included to show you how shopping around and reading labels can help you identify products that are both suitable and save you money.)

Special situations

■ Horse is otherwise healthy, but outer layer of hoof is dry and chips off easily — hooves are normal otherwise. If this horse has been exposed to topical irritants, such as drying hoof dressings, repeated shampoo baths, urine-soaked bedding, etc., this condition is likely to respond well to biotin alone, but it would be best treated by a combination product with adequate amounts of zinc and methionine added. We like **Biotin Plus-80** (Vita-Key).

■ Horse with problem hooves who is on a diet that includes regular bran feeding. If your horse receives bran more than once a week, or if bran is a major component in a prepared feed you are using, you will need to select a supplement that is not zinc-fortified. This is because the amount of zinc in bran is extremely high, which is not bad, but it does tip the zinc-to-copper ratio in the diet too heavily on the zinc end (about 7.7:1 instead of the 3:1 considered ideal).

H.B. 15 (Farnam) contains no added zinc and has adequate levels of biotin. It also has methionine and lysine, both essential amino acids, and some added vitamin B6, which is necessary for the proper utilization of proteins. However, unless the horse is on a relatively high-protein diet, the amount of amino acids it contains is probably not sufficient to make much impact.

Good shoeing is also important to good hoof health, especially for horses with problem feet.

A better choice would be **Winner's Daily**. Fed as directed, this would supply twice as much of the critical sulfur-containing amino acids and has the important added benefit of providing a generous amount of copper, which the horse on bran will need to maintain connective tissue health. The biotin level is good and the product does contain added B6.

Note: It is debatable whether horses under normal circumstances need any supplemental B6. However, under conditions of any stress, with increased protein intake and, possibly, when rebuilding injured/defective tissues, B6 requirements could rise.

The vitamin C in **Winner's Daily** is also important to connective tissue health, including the connective tissues in the foot. As an added bonus, its addition of manganese will help in maintaining normal joints.

Matching supplement to diet

1. Grass hay only — If your horse is being fed grass hay only and is eating at least 1 percent of his body weight on days when not being worked, he is already getting at least the NRC-estimated required levels of hoof-important nutrients, except for methionine. (NRC recommendations are only "best estimates" in many cases, however.) His zinc-to-copper ratio is correct. However, copper intake may be marginal, and his protein intake is also marginal. You are probably seeing the result of one or more of these factors in his feet.

For this horse, we like **Farrier's Formula** (Life Data). This product contains all the recommended nutrients for growing healthy hooves, as well as a generous amount of other important amino acids and iodine (in an appropriately conservative amount) to encourage health of the thyroid gland, which can also influence the rate of hoof growth. **Farrier's Formula** contains much less biotin (5.25 mg) than the other supplements. However, this is still almost three times the horse's basic requirement.

However, we should point out that if the horse has any type of digestive problem (constipation, diarrhea, history of colic, etc.), the levels of B vitamins available to him from his intestinal tract may be severely compromised. Since hay is not a significant source of dietary B vitamins, we feel the horse may need supplemental B, especially biotin and B6.

Vita-Key pointed out that their **Biotin Plus-80** hoof supplement was formulated so that it could be fed to horses with special needs, in combination with their **Equine Supplement** (Vita-Key) without causing imbalances in nutrients. Sure enough, a check of the combination of **Biotin Plus-80** and **Equine Supplement** shows levels of zinc, copper (as well as the ratio of zinc-to-copper) all meet or exceed those in **Farrier's Formula**. Vitamin C levels are comparable, as are those of methionine. The biotin levels are higher than for **Farrier's Formula**, and it also contains B6.

Farrier's Formula
We found Farrier's Formula comes the closest to being a complete formulation for health of the hoof and underlying connective tissues.

Winner's Daily
Winner's Daily formula is uniquely suited to the special needs of horses receiving bran as a regular part of their ration.

H.B. 15
H.B. 15 is suitable for horses on a high-quality ration who continue to have hoof problems proven by blood tests to be related to a low-biotin level.

Grand Hoof
High-potency product that meets required levels of all nutrients proven by research to affect the health of the hoof. We like the high methionine and the supplemental B6 to help the horse utilize protein.

Biotin Plus-80
Biotin Plus-80 meets the needs of otherwise healthy horses with hoof problems despite adequate diet. It can be fed combined with Vita-Key Equine Supplement to meet or exceed all minimal needs for hoof and connective tissue health.

Table of Hoof Supplement Ingredients

	Biotin Plus-80	H.B. 15	Grand Hoof	Winner's Daily*	Farrier's Formula
Biotin	15 mg	15	20	40	5.25
Methionine	1500 mg	75	3000	568.18	6188
Zinc	200 mg	—	250	trace	247
Copper	—	—	25	284.09	92
B6		20	20	18.87	—
Lysine		125	—	—	—
Vitamin C				2800	1290
Manganese				300	—
Cystine				568.18	
Sulfur				1136.36	—
Choline					487
Inositol					262
Glycine					1687
Proline					1050
Hydroxyproline					750
Trosine					618
Iodine					0.8

Note: All amounts are in mg per recommended daily dose

*Winner's Daily — partial list of ingredients, showing those of importance to hoof and connective tissue health.

We therefore feel that in this special case of a horse getting grass hay only and having a history of digestive problems, the higher biotin, additional B6 and other ingredients comparable make it a better choice for "covering all the bases." (Note: Any horse in poor condition/health may have compromised thyroid function. Ask your veterinarian to test for this possibility. If a thyroid problem is found, we suggest you ask your veterinarian to prescribe the specific supplement that suits your horse's thyroid levels.)

2. Alfalfa hay only — Horses receiving alfalfa hay only will be in better shape in terms of their protein status. However, methionine may still be deficient. Zinc status is also probably compromised, although copper levels will vary depending on the stage of the hay.

If the horse is otherwise healthy, we like **Grand Hoof** (Grand Meadows) for this horse. It contains the full daily requirement of zinc, in zinc-methionine form, as well as a modest amount of copper. Again, if the horse has a history of digestive problems, and especially if he has other connective tissue problems such as tendon or joint disease, the combination of **Biotin Plus-80** and **Equine Supplement** is your best choice.

3. Hay and grain diets — If the horse is receiving a combination of hay and grain, the situation is much more complicated. You begin with a base of the possible problems discussed above for hay only and from there must figure in the contribution of grain.

Biotin availability from grains varies widely, so you must be sure to give at least some biotin. Oats are OK for zinc but low in copper. Corn is extremely low in both. If you feed a sweet-feed mix, your zinc and copper levels will vary widely depending on the formula used. Alfalfa meal, used to boost protein, is low in both zinc and copper, while soybean meal is OK for copper but low in zinc.

If you can confirm that there are adequate copper levels in your sweet-feed mix (bare minimum of 10 ppm, 15 to 20 would probably be better), you can use **Grand Hoof.**

With marginal copper levels, however, we want to see more of it in our supplement. Your choices again are between **Farrier's Formula** or **Biotin Plus-80** combined with **Equine Supplement**. The only major difference between the two is B vitamin content. **Farrier's Formula** has no B6 and less biotin. The case against a need for excessive biotin gets a boost in the mixed-hay-and-grain diets since B vitamins are in better supply in concentrates. However, in horses with a history of digestive problems, we would go with the higher B-vitamin supplements by Vita-Key, especially if the horse has any other signs of biotin deficiency, such as dry, flaking skin.

4. Pasture-only diet — Especially when it's actively growing, fresh grass is generally a much better protein and nutrient source than plain grains or hays. However, pasture is always a mix of grasses, weeds and other plants — and that mixture can vary widely, depending on locale (soil composition, length of growing season, average temperatures and rainfall), seasonal/climate variations (drought, humidity, excessive cold or heat), and pasture management, including how often it's fertilized and mowed to encourage continued growth. So, it's virtually impossible to generalize about the nutritional values of pasture.

If your pasture-only horse is having hoof problems, first make sure his hooves are being trimmed correctly and often enough. Then, consider having your pasture analyzed for mineral composition (contact your state or local agricultural extension agent for instructions). Be sure to collect samples from spots where your horse actually grazes (horses often avoid certain areas of pasture, especially those where they tend to defecate), and take samples from multiple locations in the field, mixing them together. Then, with the resulting analysis, consult your veterinarian for advice on biotin and mineral supplementation specific to your pasture.

Summary

Hoof health is a complicated subject, with many possible nutrients playing a role. As with any nutritional problem, the makeup of the basic diet further complicates the picture.

Can any one supplement fill the needs of every individual horse, regardless of the basic diet? No. The best the companies can do is make a product that is balanced and addresses possible increased needs for certain nutrients.

To avoid hoof-health problems, begin with a proper basic diet. For balanced mineral nutrition, feed a top-quality grass hay or a mix containing about 25% alfalfa, 75% grass. Spend a little extra and buy a grain that is formulated to be balanced and meet NRC guidelines. From there, your options for supplements appropriate to use will be wider. ▪PH

For contact information on specific products mentioned, please see page 204.

Notes

17

Does Your Horse Need Iron?

Iron is essential in the horse's diet,
but in the right balance.
Iron overload can be as bad as anemia.

Geritol, One-A-Day with Iron, infant formula with iron, bread/cereals fortified with iron, Popeye's spinach — messages to "get your iron" are everywhere. Even a quick browse through most tack shops or catalogs will reveal several supplements for horses with added iron. **With regard to iron requirements, especially the use of iron supplements, human and equine needs are significantly different.**

Iron is one of the most common mineral elements in soil. **Both people and horses can obtain all the iron they need with a correct diet, eaten in sufficient amounts.** Iron is used by the body to manufacture the pigment hemoglobin, which holds oxygen inside the red blood cells. Cells need oxygen to burn important fuels obtained from the diet. Red blood cells travel throughout the body delivering a cargo of life-sustaining oxygen. Iron is also found in the muscle pigment myoglobin, which serves much the same function inside the muscle cells. The terms "anemia" and "iron-poor blood" refer to blood that contains either not enough red blood cells (in terms of their number or "blood count") or not enough hemoglobin — or both. Without a normal amount of hemoglobin, the body becomes weak. The horse also stores iron inside his bone marrow, liver and kidneys.

The horse has a large spleen, which stores far more blood cells than the spleen of many other species. The horse can mobilize these stored cells in times of stress to meet oxygen demands of heavy exercise and blood-shortage emergencies, such as might occur with a serious injury and heavy bleeding. (Note: We speak of heavy blood loss in the horse in terms of quarts or gallons. While bleeding from wounds or natural processes such as foaling may appear to be profuse, it rarely reaches amounts that could cause an iron shortage.) **Because of the horse's high natural intake of iron and efficient storage systems for this mineral, it is safe to say that horses under normal circumstances never need iron supplementation.**

Dangers of iron supplementation

Because the horse's body is so efficient at storing iron, supplementing in excess of the required levels for prolonged periods results in the build-up of toxic amounts of iron. Once iron is deposited, there is no way to get rid of it unless the body calls up iron stores to manufacture hemoglobin or myoglobin.

Some people feed extra iron, thinking it will improve the horse's red blood cell count, hemoglobin level or hematocrit (all measurements of the red blood cell system). However, supplemental iron cannot and does not have this effect. In fact, extra iron at toxic levels can actually interfere with normal blood cell production. It can also lead to abnormal liver and kidney function, and perhaps eventual failure.

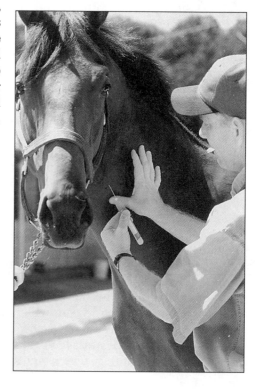

Examination of the blood, and particularly the red blood cells, can help the veterinarian determine if the horse has an iron deficiency.

Consumer tip

It is often difficult to find a mineral and vitamin supplement without iron. According to the National Research Council, the horse's daily iron requirement amounts to about 400 mg (based on an adult horse consuming 22 pounds of hay and grain, combined, per day).
Fortunately, horses who already have normal body levels of iron probably do not absorb it as well as horses who need iron. Therefore, supplements containing relatively small amounts of iron are generally safe to feed, especially if the iron is in a relatively low bioavailability form, such as iron sulfate.

Avoid chelated irons, such as iron glycineate, unless your horse has a proven iron deficiency. Do not use supplements that combine iron and vitamin C, and don't feed vitamin C and iron supplements at the same time. Vitamin C increases the absorption of iron. *However, if the C and iron are in a combined supplement, the iron will inactivate the vitamin C over time.*

Positive or negative

Long before iron reaches levels toxic enough to shut down a major organ, it causes other damage. To understand this, we need a bit of chemistry. Iron in the body carries a negative electrical charge that comes from an extra electron in the iron molecule. This means that iron is an "oxidizing substance," and it will roam around, looking to get rid of its extra electron and balance its own charges.

To do this, iron must unload its extra electron onto a molecule that was happily balanced (positive and negative charges canceling each other out) before the invading iron molecule disrupted its peace. The iron moves on in a neutral charge, but the molecule that picked up its extra electron is now in the same predicament that iron had been. It searches to balance its charge back to normal by passing the electron on to another victim.

This process will continue, damaging cells and the structures inside them, until it is squelched by a substance called an "antioxidant." Antioxidants may be vitamins (vitamin E, vitamin C), vitamin-like substances (lipoic acid) or other specialized chemicals inside the cells (glutathione).

Unfortunately, antioxidants may be in short supply and can be used up. Furthermore, there are other normal processes in the body that require antioxidants to keep them under control (i.e., white blood cells destroying invaders, or the generation of energy from foods), and the total need for antioxidants can easily exceed the supply.

Excessive iron in the diet can also interfere with the absorption of other important minerals, such as zinc and copper, and possibly calcium and magnesium. This effect, as well as the ones described earlier, can have disastrous results on many parts of the body.

What if my horse is anemic?

If blood tests indicate that your horse appears to be anemic, do not immediately reach for iron. Fit horses normally run low red blood cell counts when they are at rest, because they are efficient at using their oxygen. Red blood cells are stored in the spleen until the horse needs them. The veterinarian can check for this possibility by taking a blood sample after the horse has exercised or after giving an injection of a small amount of epinephrine, which causes the spleen to empty.

If the horse really is anemic, the characteristics of the red blood cells will help the veterinarian determine if it is really caused by an iron deficiency. Iron deficiency causes the red cells to be smaller than normal. This is measured by a test called MCV (mean cell volume). The cells will also contain less hemoglobin than normal, measured by MCH (mean cell hemoglobin). Such an anemia is extremely rare in horses, and if it occurs the veterinarian must look for a hidden cause.

If the anemia does not fit the picture of low MCV and low MCH, the cause is not iron deficiency. Among other possible causes for an anemia are: malnutrition, chronic disease, kidney disease and vitamin and mineral defi-ciencies. Other deficiencies capable of causing anemia include: B vitamins, vitamin C, vitamin E and copper. Any one of these is far more likely to be a cause of ane-mia than iron deficiency.

Iron and foals

Foals are born with low levels of iron. Analysis of mare's milk shows that it also contains relatively low levels of iron. Does this mean that foals will benefit from iron supplementation or that they will become anemic if they do not get it? No.

For one thing, the iron in mare's milk appears to be highly "bioavailable," which means that the foal can absorb it much more efficiently than iron in another form. We know that minerals combined with a protein can often be absorbed 200+ percent better than the same mineral in other forms. Minerals fed with live yeast cultures are also absorbed better than minerals in their natural form in soil or plants. The high bioavailability of the mineral means that the foal needs to receive much less of it than you would expect to get the same result.

When a foal is born, his digestive tract does not contain any bacteria. After exposure to the environment, he begins to pick up bacteria that will then either set up residence in his intestinal tract or pass on.

Whether or not a certain bacteria strain remains will depend on whether it is suited to the type of foods the foal is taking in and on other factors in the intestinal tract, such as levels of minerals that type of bacteria needs to survive.

Foals get all the iron they need from their mother's milk in a form they can utilize.

One of the most serious and potentially life-threatening diseases of foals is endotoxemia, which occurs when poisons produced by certain strains of bacteria are absorbed into the foal's bloodstream.

Nature helps protect the foal from this problem by providing the young digestive tract with an easily digested food that does not support the growth of harmful bacteria. This food is mare's milk. The bacteria required to assist digestion of milk do not require large amounts of iron to grow, but the harmful strains of bacteria do.

Interference in this design, by supplying adult types of bacteria or products containing iron, can be devastating. There are reports of foals dying within two days of receiving probiotic types of products containing high levels of iron. In these cases, autopsy confirmed classical iron poisoning.

It is therefore wise never to use iron supplements, oral or injectable, in young foals. If your veterinarian recommends use of a probiotic, it should not be started until the foal is old enough to be regularly experimenting with hay, grain and grass. You should also contact the manufacturer for further guidelines regarding when to use such products.

Iron overload case history

Our consulting veterinarian describes the case of a horse with iron overload...

This was a six-year-old gelding with assorted problems, including a history of tying up (muscular spasm and pain triggered by exercise). His skin was dry with patchy areas of hair loss in places where equipment or blankets rubbed. His coat was dry, with a reddish tinge to both the coat and the mane. His hooves were dry and brittle. Blood tests showed the horse's blood counts were in the low-to-normal range. He also had problems with inflammation and damage of the tendons and ligaments, as well as periodic filling of the tendon sheaths, which could not be easily explained by injury or excessive exercise, plus he seemed to have pain in multiple joints.

The horse was first seen after an episode of tying up. To begin treatment, the horse was given intravenous fluids containing calcium and magnesium to help relax his muscles. Several unusual things happened. The horse was tolerating large amounts of the calcium and magne-sium solution without showing any signs of toxicity. (The veterinarian must pay close attention to the heart rate when giving these fluids.) Also, the muscle spasms com-pletely relaxed, and the horse was moving around com-fortably after treatment with only the mineral solution.

This is unusual, since most horses will also require mus-cle relaxant drugs when they "tie up." The entire problem seemed to be related to a mineral imbalance. Analysis of blood taken before the horse was treated confirmed that both his calcium and magnesium levels were low. The horse also had some mild elevations in his liver enzymes and signs of mildly abnormal kidney function.

The horse's diet was checked and contained adequate amounts of calcium and magnesium, but obviously this horse would need more than he was receiving. He was treated with the antioxidants selenium and vitamin E, and was given vitamin E, vitamin C and additional calci-um and magnesium supplements.

These treatments prevented any further tying up, but the horse's magnesium and calcium levels stayed in the

The effects of iron overload will stay with a horse for life, although with treatment his hooves and coat may return to normal.

low-normal ranges and his muscle enzymes on blood tests were still abnormal. Looking for an answer that could explain the muscle, skin and hoof problems, the veterinarian did iron studies on the horse. Sure enough, the iron level was high.

The horse's current owner had not given him any iron, but a previous trainer had, probably by an iron injection as well as iron supplements in the feed. This created a huge demand for antioxidants to control damage from the reactive iron molecules. When the horse exercised, his antioxidant needs also increased (the creation of energy for exercise also generates reactive molecules). This is what caused his tying up, and the elevated muscle enzymes reflected ongoing damage every time the horse worked, even without outward signs of tying up. The extra antioxidants he was receiving were now controlling this damage, to some extent, but not preventing it entirely.

The problems with maintaining normal calcium and magnesium levels probably had two causes. On one hand, the horse was losing calcium and magnesium from damaged muscle cells (both calcium and magnesium are in high levels in muscle). There was probably also inter- ference with calcium and magnesium metabolism from the high iron. The changes in the horse's skin and coat were probably related in large part to zinc deficiency. Since iron competes with zinc and copper for absorption in the intestine, zinc and copper deficiency can occur with too much iron. His tendon, ligament and joint prob- lems could be traced to copper deficiency.

This horse will have to live with the joint, ligament and tendon damage he already has. His coat and hoof prob- lems responded well to supplementation with copper and zinc (with other nutrients, such as methionine, that he needed to rebuild healthy tissue). His tying up is con- trolled but only by heavy supplementation with antioxi- dants. Unfortunately, the iron is there to stay, and he will likely need all of this special treatment indefinitely. ▣

Section II

Raising
The Perfect Foal

18

Equine Fescue Toxicosis

Approximately 688,000 horses in the United States graze on tall fescue. Fescue toxicity has been a heartbreak for breeders, but help is on the horizon.

N o one will argue: Keeping horses is a big responsibility. When it turns out the grass in your backyard or pasture is actually highly toxic, it's an even bigger one. Such a case is possible with horses grazing fescue (*Festuca arundinacea*), a grass common especially to the southeastern United States but found in other areas also.

Fescue looks like a good choice for horses, but a serious problem lurks behind all the positive information on palatability and nutritional benefits.

Fescue toxicity

Reports of serious problems with horses grazing tall fescue grass began to appear in veterinary literature around 1980. **A mild form of fescue toxicity can be seen in horses as early as one to two weeks after fescue is fed or grazed. This is characterized by decreased weight gain, decreased milk production in nursing mares and roughened hair coats.**

The most serious form of fescue toxicity involves pregnant mares. Research studies have reported the following findings:

1. Prolonged gestation: Mares grazing toxic fescue pastures carried their foals an average of 360 days, compared to an average of 333 days for mares on nontoxic pastures.

This strong colt was born to a mare who grazed endophyte-infested fescue and received daily treatment with domperidone.

2. Death of foals: Mares grazing toxic pastures had as many as 50 percent of their foals born dead, with no stillborn foals observed in a control group of mares on nontoxic pastures.

3. Dystocia (difficult birth): In one study, mares were observed after grazing either nontoxic or toxic pastures. Of the first seven mares from the toxic pastures to foal, four had severe delivery problems and died. Six of their foals died also, though one was saved by performing a caesarean section. (The study was terminated at this point, and any remaining pregnant mares were removed from the toxic pastures.)

4. Placental abnormalities: The placentas from mares grazing toxic pastures were abnormal in weight and thickness, being an average of almost 50 percent heavier than placentas from mares grazing nontoxic pastures and almost twice as thick.

5. Retained placentas: The poisoned mares were five times more likely not to deliver their abnormal placentas after giving birth. This condition is known as retained placenta and is extremely dangerous to the mare. The retained placenta is a perfect place for bacteria to multiply rapidly. Mares can become very ill, with high fevers. Toxins produced by the bacterial growth often cause founder (laminitis). Without prompt and aggressive treatment, the mare may die.

6. Agalactia (a failure to produce milk): Of mares grazing toxic pastures, 100 percent were agalactic and unable to feed their foals.

Foals, consequently, were also unable to ingest colostrum, a mare's important first milk that provides the foal with antibodies to protect him from disease until his own immune system is mature enough to protect him. Only 12.5 percent of the mares from nontoxic pastures had any problems with milk production.

The cause of the problem

Problems of this nature naturally capture the attention of field veterinarians and researchers alike. Suspecting first a possible problem with the fescue's nutritional value, attempts were made to treat and prevent it by supplementing mares with selenium — a trace mineral known to be associated with reproductive function. This failed.

Thinking perhaps the mares were not getting adequate energy (calories), treatment was attempted by supplementing the mare's diets with an additional 50 percent of the energy requirements estimated by the NRC. This failed as well.

Investigating further, it was found that cattle grazing tall fescue pastures (tall, meaning the grass had developed seed heads) also had a variety of problems, including reduced conception rates (failure to get pregnant as readily), lower weight gains, lower milk production, rough hair coat and loss of tissue from gangrene of the feet, tail and ears.

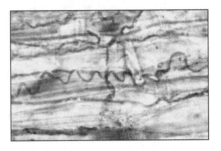

Acremonium coenophialum *is the endophyte responsible for causing problems feeding fescue.*

Researchers working on the problem in cattle had identified a fungus growing on the seed heads — *Acremonium coenophialum*. Attention was now focused on this fungus.

Tracking the fungus

The fungus found on the seed heads of fescue grass was investigated in the laboratory to see what effects it might have on various cells. This information was put together with blood work done on the mares, as well as with physical observation of placentas and mammary glands. An interesting story developed.

These weanlings were foaled at Clemson University as part of its fescue study. They are healthy and well developed.

Although all the details of the complicated biochemistry were not worked out, it was found that the mares consuming tall fescue infested with the toxic fungus had hormonal abnormalities. Their progesterone levels in late pregnancy were low, estrogen levels were too high, and prolactin was low.

Progesterone is a sex hormone that is involved in the maintenance of pregnancy. It is very high early in the pregnancy but then drops to very low levels, only to increase again in late pregnancy. The high levels in late pregnancy trigger another complicated interaction between other hormones that leads to delivery of the foal at the proper time. **It is theorized that in mares grazing infested tall fescue, abnormal progesterone levels act in conjunction with abnormalities in hormone production in the fetus to prolong pregnancy.**

The combination of higher than normal estrogen levels and lower than normal progesterone levels is responsible for the mammary glands' failure to develop in these mares. The mammary glands remain small up to and past delivery of the foal. Equally important to the mammary gland is a rise in the hormone prolactin, which normally occurs five to 10 days prior to delivery. This hormone is responsible for the mammary gland producing milk. Lowered prolactin levels in these mares resulted in the failure to produce milk.

The dystocias (difficult births) were probably caused by a combination of factors. On the one hand, proper hormone levels relax the reproductive tract, prime it for contractions and trigger the complex sequence of events that results in delivery. Abnormal hormone levels in these mares delayed that process and resulted in poor effort during labor. Another factor contributing to the dystocias was the larger size of the foals, which had been in the uterus for much longer than the normal gestation, making passage though the reproductive tract physically difficult. Abnormal positions of the legs, abnormal position of the fetus in general (lying on side, etc.) and contractions of the limbs of the unborn foal — all secondary to the prolonged time in the uterus — were among the other factors contributing to dystocia.

Patterns of outbreaks

Several factors have been identified as characteristic of fescue toxicosis in horses grazing infested pastures. Problems tend to occur sporadically but increase in number over the years. This is due to the slow spread of fungal infestation through a pasture. The fungus seems to be spread virtually entirely by infested seeds. Even within a given county, some pastures may be grazed with no problems arising, while horses on other fescue pastures nearby have difficulty, because the fungus may be infecting one pasture but not another. Reseeding a pasture with infested seeds can lead to dramatic increases in cases of toxicosis the next year. Some weather conditions, like higher temperature, also favor the growth of the fungus.

Controlling the problem

Efforts to eliminate this devastating problem may center on the pasture. Infected pastures must be destroyed and reseeded with seed that has been certified free of fungus. To slow reappearance of the problem, or dilute the toxin sufficiently to hopefully prevent recurrences, it is recommended that fescue pastures be inter-seeded with legumes (i.e., alfalfa or clover). Also, feeding supplemental hay and grain will at least decrease the severity of problems.

Hay baled from infested pastures can also result in fescue toxicity, although storing hay for a year makes it safer. **It's estimated the time for the fungus to die on hay or infested seeds could be as long as 24 months. Hay baled prior to the development of seed heads would be safe, at least theoretically.**

Pasture control measures such as these are important and should be implemented. However, they will not be 100 percent effective. The causative fungus exists in the environment and will not be eliminated simply by destroying one year's growth of infested grass. Recurrence of the problem may be delayed, but it cannot be prevented. Control measures that appear to work initially can be neutralized completely by a prolonged heat spell.

Fescue and young horses

Although problems of slowed/poor growth have been reported in young horses grazing fescue pastures, they do not seem to be related to toxicity from fungal endophyte infestation. The nutritional value of a pasture, particularly its calorie and protein levels, drops sharply at certain times of the year. Unless the grass is in a rapid-growth stage, the nutrient level may be insufficient for young, growing horses. Supplementing with grain and a high-quality hay will correct the problem. Mowing pastures before they reach the tall, seed-head stage will also ensure that the youngsters get a stage of growth with greater nutritional value, but supplementation with grain and hay will still likely be necessary, especially at times of the year when the grass is dormant.

Controlling and treating fescue toxicity

Various methods of pasture management have been tried in efforts to keep pastures safe for mares throughout their pregnancy. However, results have been largely disappointing or far too expensive to consider on a routine basis.

For instance, special endophyte-free strains of fescue have been developed. One method of pasture management calls for complete destruction of the existing pasture with a herbicide, then reseeding with endophyte-free strains. Unfortunately, the problem often returns rather quickly, as either the endophyte-free fescues lose their resistance and/or seeds from neighboring infected pastures make their way into the reseeded areas.

A similar approach with somewhat better results has been to reseed, after the herbicide treatment, with a mixture of orchard grass, rye, bluegrass and red clover or other dense-growth grasses (called

*This mare was treated with domperidone while grazing fescue.
She delivered a live, healthy foal and had lots of milk.*

"choke crops," because they form a thick network at ground level
and tend to choke out the growth of other grasses). Using a seed mixture such as this will produce safe pastures for about two to three
years, after which the entire process must be repeated. Also, the pastures cannot be grazed during the years they are being treated and
reseeded.

For most farms, the above methods are far more trouble and expense than they are worth. Other management options focus on the
mares themselves. **Removing mares from fescue pastures 30 to 90
days prior to their expected foaling date and feeding them fescue-
free hay and grain during that period results in normal mammary
development, normal placentas and normal foaling times.** The 30-
day figure has been reported as accurate, although many people pull
their mares off pasture before this "just to be safe." Mares can be
kept on a dry lot during this time or, if absolutely necessary, kept in
stalls. Even a small dry lot is preferable, however, as sunlight is important to health, and the mare should have enough room to walk
about freely and roll if she wants to. Remember to keep stalls and
small lots meticulously clean, dry and free of manure. Mares will
not foal in a "dirty" area.

If this isn't an option either, mares can be treated with the drug
domperidone (available as a paste), beginning 10 to 14 days prior

to the expected foaling date. **Domperidone reverses the chemical block in the production of key hormones such as prolactin (the milk production hormone) and allows the pregnancy to proceed normally.** Domperidone must be prescribed by, and its use supervised by, your veterinarian. Getting the correct dosage can be a little tricky: Mares may require different dosages depending on their own hormonal variations, as well as on the level of endophyte contamination in their pastures (it is possible to test and determine your pasture's level of endophyte infestation by contacting Dr. Dee Cross at Clemson University; see page 204 for contact information). Your veterinarian will observe the mare's response and adjust her dosage as necessary.

For mares whose milk production is still poor after foaling, the drug can be continued for up to 10 days. Veterinarians using domperidone before and after foaling report excellent results. ■PH■

19

Problem Broodmares

*Sometimes, getting a mare in foal
isn't as easy as it sounds. Some experts blame
specific physical problems, and others
place the emphasis on general health and nutrition.*

Probably the most common reason for mares failing to conceive is a lack of nutrition or poor general condition. The stress of the preceding foaling and then producing milk usually causes mares to lose a considerable amount of weight. In this "catabolic" condition, the mare burns her own fat and muscle reserves to generate calories, first for growing the foal and then for producing milk, putting the mare in a "negative energy balance." The result is a poor conception rate.

However, mares who have recently foaled aren't the only ones with this problem. "Open" or non-pregnant mares who are fed poor-quality diets over the winter, and who enter the spring breeding season in extremely poor condition (in terms of body weight and vitamin/mineral status), have poor conception rates. **Underfeeding of non-pregnant mares is such a widespread practice that poor-quality hay is sometimes referred to as "broodmare hay."**

Stress is another influence on overall health and, potentially, on fertility. Mares who are shipped from their familiar surroundings to a breeding farm — and turned out into a large group of unfamiliar mares — are highly stressed. Weight loss is common, as is nervousness from the pressure of adapting to the group. Minor fights break out frequently, and competition for food and water may be fierce. Only the strongest mares can tolerate this type of challenge and remain unscathed. For most, the psychological and physical stress often results in failure to conceive.

Considering the work and expense of choosing a stallion and preparing your mare for breeding, it's important to understand potential conception problems.

For mares coming to the breeding farm after a season of intensive competition, the situation is even worse, since the stress of showing or racing often depletes physical reserves.

Physical problems

If you are at all familiar with breeding horses, you have heard of a Caslick's repair. This simple procedure sews shut the top half of the mare's vaginal lips. Caslick's repairs help prevent reproductive-tract infections caused by fecal material entering the vagina, and they prevent "wind sucking" (air being drawn into the vagina when the mare exercises).

Although there are valid reasons for performing a Caslick's, common sense alone will tell you that not all mares need to have their vaginas sewn shut to prevent their reproductive tract from getting "infected." However, in some locales, Caslick's repairs are performed far too frequently on mares who do not need the surgery. In fact, it is common practice on some breeding farms to have every mare "sewn shut" once she is confirmed to be in foal.

It is also common in some areas to blame reproductive-tract infections as the cause for any mare who does not conceive — treatment, of course, being to perform a Caslick's operation, after treating with an antibiotic, and then to try breeding her again. Do not accept this explanation without further investigation. The vagina is not normally sterile; instead, it typically contains various levels and types of bacteria at all times. However, cultures collected from the vagina and cervix, using strict sterile technique, can confirm or disprove any suspicion of a real infection.

PROBLEMS WITH THE OVARIES ARE RARE, ALTHOUGH A FEW MARES MAY START TO DEVELOP FOLLICLES THAT NEVER FULLY MATURE AND RELEASE AN EGG.

Injuries sustained in a prior foaling may create breeding problems. A damaged cervix may heal in a scarred position that either blocks the passage of sperm (rare) or prevents the cervix from opening and closing normally. A cervix that will not close tightly cannot seal off the uterus (which is normally free of organisms) from the vagina (which is not bacteria-free). A mare with this problem will be more prone to developing uterine infections and early abortions.

If a culture is needed, the veterinarian will either wait until her next "heat" period or use drugs to open the mare's cervix enough to collect samples. Special specimen-taking devices hold the collecting swab inside a sterile plastic tube that is threaded through the cervix and into the uterus. The vet then pushes on the end of the culture swab to release its tip inside the uterus. The tip is pulled safely back into the interior of the tube before the assembly is withdrawn. Most mares tolerate this procedure well.

If treatment is needed, antibiotics (sometimes mixed in saline) are infused directly into the uterus using a rubber or plastic tube. Mares with a large collection of material (puss and dead tissues) inside the uterus will need to have these contaminants flushed out before the antibiotics can go to work. Two or three treatments will be done, every day or every other day. Some veterinarians leave the tubing coiled inside the uterus and exiting the vagina for the several-day treatment period. A repeat culture will be done at the time of the mare's next estrus (heat). Once the infection has cleared, the vet may recommend a biopsy of the interior of the uterus to check for microscopic scarring.

Scarring inside the uterus can also have negative effects on fertility. A badly scarred uterus may prevent a fertilized egg from implanting. If the uterine wall is less severely damaged, the egg may implant and grow for a time, but when the fetus needs to expand over large areas of the placenta in order to absorb enough nutrition, it will be unable to do so, and abortion results. All of this can occur before the mare was even known to be pregnant, and there may be no external signs to tell you she had lost a microscopic fetus.

Problems with the ovaries are rare, although a few mares may start to develop follicles that never fully mature and release an egg. This cycle irregularity most commonly occurs very early or very late in the breeding season. Rectal examination of the mare close to the time she should be in estrus may help uncover this problem.

The stallion

Just as it takes two to tango, it takes two to make a foal, and "dad" may be the one to blame for "mom" not becoming pregnant. When choosing a stallion, whether a big-name or backyard horse, on a large breeding operation or small farm, make sure you ask questions about his fertility.

Large breeding operations routinely check the semen of their stallion for sperm count, sperm deformities and sperm vigor/motility. **What you need to know is the bottom line — how many mares he bred over the last year (or few years), and how many mares were confirmed in foal.** If you cannot get this information, pick another stallion or realize that you are taking your chances with an unproven sire.

Another useful tidbit is how many times the mares were bred, on average, before they conceived. A stallion with decreased fertility may be able to get a mare in foal if he tries over several heat periods, succeeding when the timing is exactly right. However, this can greatly increase expenses for the mare owner, in terms of long periods of boarding at the stud farm or multiple shipping and veterinary fees.

Mares who may need a Caslick's

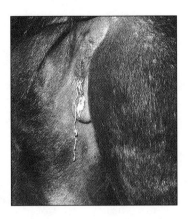

In the normal mare, the vagina is oriented perpendicular to the ground and the anal opening. When the mare passes manure, it falls directly to the ground without contacting the vagina. Some mares (usually older mares) have insufficient support to these structures; the result is that the anus "sinks in" somewhat and the top portion of the vagina angles back more in line with the horse's spine, making the vagina "tipped" inward. With this conformation, fecal material may indeed enter the vagina and cause an infection.

"Sucking air," however, is not necessarily associated with obvious anatomical abnormalities. Instead, it can be detected when the veterinarian does a vaginal examination and finds tiny bubbles (usually in traces of urine) inside the vagina.

A third problem, found in mares with a "tipped" vagina, is pooling of urine in the vagina. When the mare urinates, she is unable to force all the urine to the outside. The vagina then becomes a breeding place for bacteria. While this problem can indeed cause fertility problems, it is not corrected by a Caslick's. A special surgery is needed to bring the urethra forward into a more normal position.

Ship in or board

Consider boarding your mare at the breeding farm for a few days prior to the anticipated breeding date (and ask that she be kept in a stall, not out in the broodmare field). If you wait to ship the mare until she is showing strong estrus and/or has a large follicle on rectal examination, you run the risk that she will ovulate (release the

Broodmare supplementation

***Begin optimizing the mare's
nutrition at least three months
prior to the time of breeding.***

*Studies have shown that sup-
plementation with vitamin A
can improve fertility in the
early breeding season. (Keep
those carrots coming!) It is a
well-known fact that vitamin A
levels drop considerably during
the winter and are lower all
year in horses fed hays but
denied access to pasture.
However, oversupplementation
with vitamin A (longer than six
months) could cause toxicity. It
is currently recommended that
high vitamin A/beta carotene
(the vitamin A precursor)* may be beneficial when begun
approximately three months prior to breeding season
and continued until the mare has conceived or again
has access to high-quality pasture, at which time it
should be discontinued.*

*Vita-Key's Broodmare
Supplement is specially
formulated to provide
the vitamin A, B-vita-
mins and trace miner-
als needed for opti-
mum fertility.*

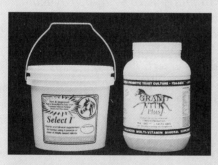

*Select I (Select The Best) or
Grand Vite (Grand Meadows) is
appropriate for mares receiving
alfalfa hay only.*

*Vitamin A is of spe-
cial concern, but
other trace minerals
and vitamins are also
important. We rec-
ommend you keep
the mare on a diet of
the best-quality hay
you can find, fed at a
level of at least one
percent of her body
weight (10 pounds a
day for a 1,000-
pound horse) with a*

multivitamin-and-mineral supplement designed to complement the hay.

If the mare can stay in good flesh on hay alone (this means ribs not visible and just barely able to be felt), use a vitamin-and-mineral supplement that provides calcium and phosphorus in ratios that balance the hay — more calcium than phosphorus (between 1.5:1 to 2.0:1) for grass hays; more

Equi-Base (Uckele) can be used to supplement mares on grass-hay based diets.

phosphorus than calcium for alfalfa hay (0.5:1 to 1:1).

If feeding a mixed hay at a rate of at least one percent of body weight, you do not need to be concerned about calcium and phosphorus and can use a supplement that does not contain these minerals. If small amounts of grain must be fed to maintain body weight, you can use the same guidelines as above in picking a supplement — that is, match the supplement to the hay.

RECOMMENDED BROODMARE SUPPLEMENTATION
(1,000 lb. body weight; mid-bloom cutting hays)

DIET	SUPPLEMENTS
Alfalfa hay only, 1% of body weight (about 11 lbs.)	High phosphorus supplement, such as Select I*, or 1/2 pound of bran daily with Broodmare Supplement
Alfalfa hay only, 1% of body weight with 2-3 pounds of grain	Select I or Broodmare Supplement
Mixed hay, with or without grain	Broodmare Supplement
Grass hay only, 1% of body weight (about 11 lbs.)	Balanced Ca:Ph supplement, such as Select II (Select The Best) or Equi-Base
Free-choice grass hay, or grass hay with 2-3 pounds of grain	Broodmare Supplement or Select II

*Grand Vite may be substituted for Select I

Companionship is sometimes a helpful factor — mares who live together often cycle at the same time.

egg) during shipping or immediately after she arrives at the breeding farm. If she is not examined and "teased" (tested for how receptive to the stallion she is) until the day after arrival, you may miss the opportunity to breed on that cycle.

Management at the breeding farm

How the actual breeding is handled can also influence how likely the mare is to conceive. If you are starting with a normal healthy mare and stallion, the best way to get her in foal is to turn them out together and leave them alone! Many people feel this is too risky when valuable animals are involved (the stallion is more likely to be injured than the mare) and insist that breeding be done "in hand," with the mare restrained and a person handling the stallion. This is the next-best method to turn-out and is often successful, as long as the stallion is not rushed or abused by his handler.

Management policies, such as artificial insemination and breeding mares based on the results of rectal examinations to palpate their ovaries for follicles, may lower conception rates instead of improving them when these examinations are spaced out to every other day or even a three-day gap over weekends. This is particularly a problem on large farms where only a limited number of mares can be inseminated any given day. In that situation, mares that are felt (really an educated guess) to be closest to ovulating will be bred. If yours is one of the ones not bred and she happens to ovulate right before her next palpation, you will be waiting another three weeks for cover, even if the mare still shows strong signs of estrus.

When considering a certain breeding farm, ask:

- How are the mares and stallions handled?
- Who decides when and how many times a mare will be bred?
- How is that decision made?
- How are the mares booked to that particular stallion handled, since there are often differences between stallion handlers even on the same farm?
- How many mares were bred to the stallion last year?
- How many were confirmed in foal?
- How many "covers" (breedings) did it take the stallion to get those mares in foal?

What can you do?

If your mare has known breeding problems or if you want to avoid them, first look for physical problems that could influence fertility. Have the mare examined by a veterinarian who does a great deal of breeding work (there's no substitute for experience!). Uterine cultures and even biopsies, which are considered routine tests in many circumstances, may be recommended.

If you question something the veterinarian tells you, get a second opinion. This can be money well spent; it's certainly far less than you stand to lose if the problem isn't correctly identified, and you invest in shipping, boarding and breeding to no avail.

Your mare should be in the best possible health at breeding time, which means she must be of normal weight (or perhaps with even a slight reserve of body fat for energy), and she should have normal vitamin and mineral levels. Keep in mind that winter — the months immediately preceding the breeding season — is the worst nutritional time of the year for horses. Hay and grain are a poor substitute for adequate pasture, both in terms of nutrients and digestibility.

If you will be boarding your mare at a breeding farm, ask about the type of diet she'll receive, to see if it's different from her diet at home. If so, ask if the breeding farm will honor individual requests. If they don't, make gradual changes in what you normally feed until she is accustomed to a diet similar to the one she will receive at the farm — and make those changes well in advance of going there.

To minimize the negative impact of stress, choose your breeding farm carefully. Visit the farm and observe how the mares are kept and what condition they are in. If you do not like the mare management on the farm but really want to use a particular stallion, inquire about outlying farms where you can board and have your mare shipped in to be bred. This will mean a little more expense and trouble. On the other hand, it may mean a better chance that the mare will conceive and conceive more quickly. **PH**

For contact information on specific products mentioned, please see page 204.

20

Basic Guide To Foaling

*After an 11-month wait, the birth of a foal
is miraculous and nerve-wracking at the same time.
We'll tell you what happens and how to be prepared.*

The birth of a foal is exciting and awe-inspiring to witness, whether it is your first or you are an old pro. In most cases, the process occurs fairly smoothly with no need for human intervention. However, it is always best to be well-informed about the birthing process and prepared for a complicated delivery. There are also several things you should do in the critical first few hours after birth to make sure the foal gets off to a good start.

Preparation

Beginning at least three months before foaling, be sure that your mare's diet contains sufficient levels of protein (especially the amino acid lysine) and minerals (especially calcium, phosphorus, copper and zinc) — at least meeting NRC recommendations.

At least one month in advance of the due date, the mare should be moved into her foaling quarters and should be using the same turnout facilities she will use after the birth of the foal. This allows her body adequate time to develop antibodies to bacteria in the area, in order to pass these along to the foal in her colostrum. It also allows her time to adjust to being separated from her buddies.

At this time, she should also be vaccinated and, a few days before changing her stall, dewormed. Make sure that any horses who will be in the barn or who will be using the same turnout are up to

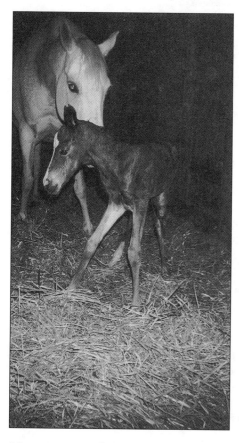

Most mares and foals are up within about an hour of foaling without help from an attendant.

date on vaccinations and deworming, also.

The foaling stall itself should be roomy, at least 12 x 12 feet, but preferably larger. Go over every inch of the walls carefully for protruding nails, loose splinters of wood, loose metal edging and so forth. If there is anything in the stall that could cause an injury, there's a good chance the foal will find it. Water and feed buckets should be well-secured.

Bed the stall in straw instead of shavings. There is less chance of harmful bacteria breeding with straw than on shavings. During foaling, the mare may be up and down, the foal partly protruding from her body, then receding into her body. Shavings could stick to the foal and be taken back into the mare's body.

If possible, don't place another horse in a stall next to her, even a good buddy, at least for the first week or two after the birth. **Mares are extremely protective of their foals, especially in the period immediately after birth.** She will likely spend a great deal of time threatening the neighbor and trying to keep the baby at a distance, sometimes to the point that she will not eat, drink or rest well. If necessary, you can nail up a piece of plywood to separate the stalls.

It is also a good idea to put together a foaling kit at least two weeks in advance of the delivery date.

Beginning two weeks before the due date, the mare's tail should be wrapped nightly. The tail-wrapping material in your kit can be any non-stretchy fabric you are comfortable using and should be long enough to include the entire tail. Some people prefer to use rolls of gauze, throwing them away after use. However, this can get expensive, and we find regular leg bandages with hook-and-loop closures work very well. These can be washed after each use.

The purpose of wrapping the tail is to prevent it from becoming heavily soiled during the birth and then serving as a place for bacteria to grow in close proximity to the genital area. It is also difficult to keep tail hair out of the way if the mare needs to be examined or assisted.

After wrapping the tail each night, you should also gently wash the area of the skin of the vaginal opening and around the anus. This does not by any means sterilize it but helps remove large clumps of dirt or fecal material that could contribute to infection of the reproductive tract after foaling.

Talk to your veterinarian in advance of the expected foaling date. If you decide to have the veterinarian present for the delivery, ask when he or she should be called. Fortunately, most minor difficulties during delivery are easily corrected with a little assistance from the foaling attendant (you) as described below, but when professional help is necessary, timing can be critical.

Understanding natural changes

During the last month of pregnancy, the mare will show some changes. She will gradually become more withdrawn, both from you and other horses. This is partially a result of being uncomfortable with the large foal and partially a natural instinct to isolate herself as foaling approaches.

Mares in late pregnancy commonly have periods in which they do not eat particularly well and may even appear mildly uncomfortable or colicky. This is a result of pressure being put upon the intestines by the large uterus. This is not a cause for panic unless the mare appears to be in severe pain (blowing, sweating, pawing, lying down) or she refuses to eat and drink. Greatly reduced amounts of manure or failure to pass manure for a few hours could also indicate a more serious problem. In those cases, a veterinarian should be called to determine if an examination is necessary.

In addition to ensuring that your mare receives immediate help if she needs it, your careful account of the details may make the difference between the veterinarian making an unnecessary ranch call or just giving you advice via telephone consultation about what to do and watch for.

Foaling kit

This should include:

- Towels
- Mild soap
- String and scissors
- Small bucket
- Sponge
- Plastic gloves
- Carryall large enough to hold the supplies
- K-Y or other lubricant jelly
- Tail-wrapping material
- Rectal examination sleeves

- Betadine, Povidone or other skin-friendly iodine solution and a small cup

Predicting foaling

Unfortunately, calendar predictions are no more accurate for horses than for people. Most breeders estimate the foaling date by taking the last date the mare was bred and adding 11 months to it. This is only an approximation. Even in a normal pregnancy, this date can easily be off by several weeks.

Mares carry their foals for anywhere from 320 to about 360 days. Horses usually require a minimum of 330 days of pregnancy to ensure adequate maturity of the foal. The most common length of pregnancy is around 340 days, which will put the mare's foaling at about two weeks past the 11-month estimation.

For example, if she is bred May 5, 11 months later puts the foaling date at April 5. The actual foaling date will probably be in the teens. You may be able to predict dates more accurately if the mare has had several other foals and you can get the breeding and foaling dates. If she has carried her previous pregnancies for approximately the same number of days each time, she is likely to do so again.

The mare will also undergo several physical changes as foaling time approaches. The udder will begin to swell with edema and milk. A yellowish substance will appear on the ends of the teats. This is called "waxing" and is likely to occur within 48 hours of foaling. The teats themselves will swell a few hours before foaling.

These signs are fairly reliable indicators, but there are individual variations.

Maiden mares may not show as much udder development, while mares who have foaled several times may show a swollen udder several weeks in advance of the foaling and, for days to weeks before foaling, may even drip milk.

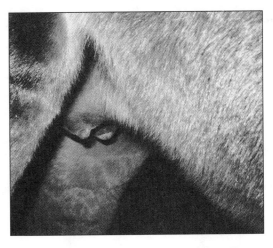

Prior to foaling, the mare's udder will swell. This may not be very pronounced in first-time pregnancies.

The area around the base of the tail and the large muscles of the rump will become soft and flattened, due to relaxation of the ligaments of the pelvis. This can be seen by viewing the mare directly from behind or by feeling the area. Changes become evident a week or so in advance of foaling and will be most noticeable just before foaling.

As the pelvic ligaments relax, the vaginal area begins to undergo changes. It becomes swollen and relaxed, lengthening to as much as twice the normal size just before foaling.

As these physical changes occur, the mare may become progressively more irritable or agitated. Appetite, especially for grain, often drops off somewhat, although the mare may eventually eat all her grain if it is left in front of her long enough. A complete refusal of grain and signs of increased agitation often signal that foaling is imminent.

Unfortunately, none of these predictors is accurate, although taken together they may alert you within a few days of foaling.

The watch begins

The foaling process in horses is normally rapid and may be violent. The mare develops pressures during contractions strong enough to fracture a man's arm if he is doing an examination and it becomes trapped against the pelvis during a contraction. Because of this, a foal that is malpositioned in such a way that the umbilical cord becomes shut down during contractions can easily die or suffer permanent injury due to the loss of blood supply. This is why it is common practice to watch the mare closely during late pregnancy and make every effort to have someone present during labor.

In the case of a mare with an unknown foaling history, or with a maiden (first-time pregnant) mare, watches usually begin at about the 320-day mark. Mares are checked every one to two hours throughout the night and occasionally during the day. Even this frequent a check may allow a normal foaling to be missed, but careful attention to the mare should result in detection of a problem birth in time to get her some help.

MARES WHO DO NOT DELIVER THEIR ENTIRE PLACENTA WITHIN APPROXIMATELY TWO HOURS ARE AT HIGH RISK FOR A LIFE-THREATENING UTERINE INFECTION AND LAMINITIS (FOUNDER).

When mares have a history of foaling problems, watches should also begin early and be done at least every hour. It may be advisable to consult with your veterinarian about the possibility of inducing the labor in such mares. While this can have its own special problems, especially if done too early, induction has the advantage of timing the birth so that the veterinarian can be present.

Generally, watches should begin when pelvic ligament relaxation becomes evident and vaginal changes start to occur.

When it seems that foaling is imminent, remove feed and water buckets and anything projecting from the walls that could injure a foal should the mare bump into them during foaling. After foaling, however, you can replace them.

You should also look at your watch when foaling actually starts. It's easy to lose track of time, and two minutes can seem like 20 when you are waiting for something to happen.

Most mares lie down to deliver their foals; in fact, a mare who insists on standing and forcibly straining may be doing so because the foal is not positioned properly.

It is common for mares to push a few times standing, lie down, get up again and even roll before lying down for the actual delivery. This may be due to agitation or to efforts to get the foal in a better position. Do not interfere unless the mare has been obviously straining for 10 minutes or longer and/or if a part of the foal becomes visible but retracts repeatedly without progress. If this is the case, call the veterinarian.

Stages of labor

Labor occurs in three stages — early labor, strong labor and delivery, and expulsion of the afterbirth (placenta). Early signs of labor may be quite subtle, with some mares showing no obvious signs at all. As a general rule, maiden mares show more signs in early labor, while experienced mares show fewer. For both, however, these signs become more obvious and dramatic as delivery approaches and the strength of contractions increases.

Signs include:
- *Agitation, pacing.*
- *Decreased appetite.*
- *Frequent passage of small amounts of urine and manure.*
- *Light sweating, which may become pronounced.*
- *Signs of abdominal pain — pawing, kicking at belly, looking around at belly.*

When to help

It is *NOT* necessary to "help" the mare during a normal delivery. Normal deliveries are usually accomplished after only a few good, hard pushes and will take about 20 minutes.

While it only takes a minute to put gloves on, you should have your foaling supplies right outside the stall door. The long rectal examination sleeves should be put on first, with tight-fitting rubber or plastic gloves on top. Pour Betadine/iodine solution over the gloves to disinfect them.

Foals are normally delivered front end first. The first thing that appears is either a foot or the white sac containing the foal (this is called the "amnion"). The sole of the foot will usually be facing the ground but can rotate during the early part of the delivery.

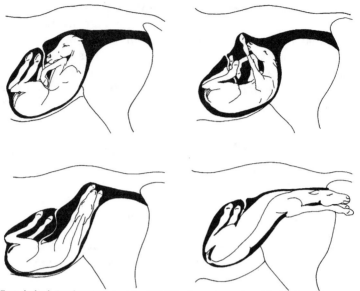

From the book, Breeding Management and Foal Development, *courtesy of Equine Research 800-848-0225*

During the first stages of foaling, the fetus gradually shifts from a position on its back, rotating until its head and forelimbs are extended in the birth canal.

The next thing you will see is the other foot, followed closely by the nose. The head emerges resting on the forelegs. If only one foot and a nose or both feet and no nose are seen after repeated pushes by the mare, she needs veterinary help.

If the front feet and nose are visible, but the mare is not making much progress, you can carefully assist (after putting on gloves) by grasping the front feet and pulling down toward the mare's hocks during contractions. It is essential to maintain this downward direction of pull and to pull only when the mare is actively pushing.

If the foal does not budge, you will need veterinary assistance immediately. Keeping the mare on her feet until help arrives will help the foal drop back into a safe position in the uterus. If you see only one foot, one foot and a nose, or both feet but no nose, the foal may be malpositioned, so DO NOT PULL. This type of improper positioning must be corrected by someone experienced, or severe injury to the mare could easily occur.

If the foal is being delivered hind-end first (which you will know if the soles of his feet are facing toward the ceiling and stay in that position), the mare may need immediate assistance unless the birth proceeds rapidly on its own. The foal's abdomen and chest can be compressed somewhat, but the shoulders cannot. This is the largest part of the foal, and if it becomes wedged in the pelvis, the umbilical cord can become compressed, shutting off critical oxygen to the foal.

Wait until the foal's hindquarters are free, and you can see a good bit of the chest (do not pull before this point). Then, if the mare has given a push or two without making progress, grasp the foal's hind feet or hocks and, as described above, pull down toward the mare's hocks during contractions. The foal may be positioned a little bit off to one side or the other. If you need to pull, do not try to straighten the foal first. This slight positioning to one side or the other may help the shoulders slip through easier, allowing one to progress a little bit in front of the other. **Always time your pulls to work with the mare's own pushing. Do not pull between contractions.**

When the foal is malpositioned or the foaling is taking more than 20 minutes, experienced help is needed.

The newborn foal

The foal will normally rupture the very thin amnionic sac in the process of passing through the birth canal. If this has not occurred by the time his upper forelegs are beginning to appear, you may open a small hole in the sac over the foal's nostrils (you will be able to see the foal clearly through the thin membrane).

The pressures generated during the birth are usually quite effective in forcing any fluid out of the foal's chest and upper airway. Immediately after birth, there may be some frothy fluid around the nose and mouth.

The foal will normally deal with this by snorting. If the foal seems very tired or depressed and if the fluid is excessive, you can gently wipe it away with a towel. If there are obvious loud gurgling noises and fluid continues to appear, you can roll the foal into a position where he is resting on his sternum (breastbone).

If this does not help and the foal seems distressed (head and neck extended, mouth open, working hard to breathe), try elevating the hindquarters while the foal remains resting on his sternum with his front legs bent, to encourage the fluids to drain. (Note: You will need three people, two with the foal — one at the front, one at the rear — and someone with the mare.)

If the foal resists so vigorously that you have trouble getting him to remain in this position, chances are he's doing just fine anyway and doesn't need that level of help. To be safe, call the veterinarian.

Important DON'TS during foaling

- *Don't even enter the stall unless you are absolutely needed.*

- *Don't pull on the foal if the mare is making progress.*

- *Don't cut the cord unless it is under excessive tension.*

- *Don't attempt to force the foal to nurse.*

- *Don't towel off the foal.*

- *Don't assist the foal to his feet.*

- *Don't use flash bulbs if taking photos.*

- *Don't attempt to pull out the placenta.*

- *Don't leave the mare and foal alone until the foal has gotten to his feet and successfully nursed.*

- *Don't hesitate to call the veterinarian if problems with either the mare or the foal have resulted in the foal's not nursing within two hours of birth.*

The normal foal

It is often difficult for people to tell if a foal is "normal." Poor balance, wobbling on his feet, banging into walls and falling down are all normal, and the foal will begin to show much more coordination in a day or so. The important thing is that he is trying and keeps trying.

The foal's breathing and heart rate will usually be rapid, both because this is normal for a young animal and also because of the excitement and the effort involved in "finding his legs."

The rest periods between efforts to stand and walk may vary widely. If you think the foal is staying down too long or seems to be "dopey," there are a few quick things you can check.

Put a finger into his ear. He should respond by shaking his head or twitching the ear. Put your finger into his mouth. This should

Normal foals are alert and responsive to the mare and to noises or movements in their environment.

trigger a strong sucking response. He should respond to sharp sounds, such as you clapping your hands. As you approach, the foal should seem interested, looking in your direction and probably extending his muzzle.

As a general rule, the foal will have recovered enough from the trauma of birth by the time the mare has recovered, and vice versa. If the foal remains down for more than an hour and is listless or does not respond to the quick tests above, call the veterinarian.

After delivery

Usually the mare and foal are exhausted and will normally remain lying down for at least 15 minutes, perhaps as long as 30 minutes after foaling. Most mares will be up before this time, nosing and licking their foal.

If the mare remains down, especially if the foal is already up or trying to get up, and she seems uninterested in the foal or anything going on around her, or if she is breathing heavily and sweating, showing signs of either distress or depression, get the veterinarian immediately.

Normally, the mare will look back and nicker to the foal, licking him if he is within reach. The foal will often scramble in the direction of the mare's voice. During this time, the umbilical cord may remain attached. Do NOT tie and cut the umbilical cord for the first 15 to 20 minutes. The cord will usually break on its own.

The blood remaining in the mare's placenta is drained into the foal through the umbilical cord during this period, and cutting it too soon will deprive him of part of his blood. **Once the blood has passed into the foal, neither mare nor foal will hemorrhage when the cord separates.**

Tying off the umbilical cord

Cut a piece of string about eight inches long and, using a square knot, tie off the umbilical cord about two inches from the foal's belly. With another piece of string, tie another square knot about two inches closer to the mare than the first. Cut between the two knots.

Stage three of labor

Foals orphaned at birth have special needs and require careful attention and frequent feeding.

The mare will again push and deliver the placenta, a large red blob. This normally occurs within a few minutes of the foal's birth. In some cases, only part of the placenta will be seen emerging from the vagina, and complete delivery may take a few hours.

If the mare does not deliver (expel) the entire placenta within a few minutes, allow it to remain where it is. Do NOT pull on the placenta. This can tear the placenta, leaving a piece of it behind and causing serious problems.

Mares who do not deliver their entire placenta within approximately two hours are at high risk for a life-threatening uterine infection and laminitis

(founder). When the placenta is delivered, spread it out on the ground. It will be in the shape of a "Y." One of the upper limbs of the "Y" will be larger than the other; this is the side of the uterus where the foal developed. There will be a hole in the placenta where it ruptured and the foal passed through.

If you suspect or can't tell if a piece is missing, save the placenta in a bucket or plastic bag (away from other barn animals) and as soon as possible have a veterinarian examine it, definitely within eight to 12 hours. If the placenta is not delivered within two hours, call the veterinarian.

Standing-up delivery

In the rare event of a mare foaling while standing up (more common in maiden mares than experienced ones), there is a lot of tension on the umbilical cord. Not only is there a risk of the foal bleeding should the umbilical cord rip, but the mare may bleed or her placenta tear and a piece of the placenta end up inside her.

A standing birth can be a normal birth in every other way, but there are some precautions you should take. Position a helper at the mare's head to prevent her walking, and get in position to catch the foal, to break its fall.

If the umbilical cord is under tension, tie it off as described below and cut it. If the cord is sufficiently long to not be under tension and the mare does not strenuously resist standing still, wait at least 10 to 20 minutes before tying and cutting the cord and releasing the mare. If the mare becomes too agitated at any point, proceed with tying and cutting the cord.

After-delivery care

If everything goes well, you won't even enter the stall until after the umbilical cord has separated. The stump of the umbilical cord should be dipped into Betadine/iodine placed in a small cup. (Dosing cups from cold medications are an ideal size for this.) If you are putting iodine on the end while the foal is lying down, be sure you reach across his back so as not to get kicked.

There is no need to towel off the foal, even if the foal shivers for a few minutes. The mare will normally lick him clean and dry, and this is an important part of the bonding process. However, if the mare seems exhausted and does not attend to the foal within 30 minutes or so, you can towel him off, at least partially. Allow the mare to smell the towel to identify her foal and to assist bonding.

You should then get out of the stall and just observe the mare and foal. Both will get to their feet within an hour or so of foaling, most mares getting up within minutes. After the foal "finds his legs" he will urinate, pass the first manure (called meconium) and actively seek to nurse, not necessarily in that order. You should observe the pair until the foal has accomplished all of this.

With male foals, pay particular attention to urination. In some males, the connection between penis and bladder is not formed, and urine will come out the umbilical area. This requires immediate veterinary attention. You will also need the veterinarian if the foal strains but does not pass meconium or if he seems weak or has not successfully nursed within two hours of birth.

Most mares are committed mothers, some to the point of aggressively attacking any animal or person who attempts to come what she thinks is too close. Immediately after foaling, she will be too tired to worry about this for a while, but she could become aggressive without warning at any time, so be alert.

Some mares do not properly care for their foals. The first sign of this is failure to lick the foal clean. Later on, the mare may push the foal away or even kick at it. You may need professional help to deal with this problem, also.

Maiden mares may not readily accept the foal's attempts to nurse, even though they seem interested in the foal otherwise. This is due sometimes to inexperience and sometimes to discomfort. If the foal is strong and eagerly seeking to nurse, having someone stand at the mare's head until the foal has a chance to nurse may be all that is needed.

Be patient and do not otherwise interfere with the actions of the foal. If this does not work after two hours, again you will need professional assistance — especially to make sure the foal gets adequate colostrum in those first few critical hours.

After the foal has nursed, defecated and urinated, you have your most difficult task to do — leave the two alone to rest! ▣

21

The Orphaned Foal

*Knowledge and good preparation can make
a life-or-death difference if your foal is orphaned
or if your mare doesn't produce enough colostrum.*

F ew things are more tragic for horse owners than a foal losing its mother — and few things are more difficult than raising an orphaned foal. If your mare is pregnant, or if you are
thinking of breeding, it is wise to make some advance prepa-
rations and understand fully what must be done should the foal become an orphan. Undoubtedly, it will be an emotional time for you,
but timing may be critical in saving the foal's life.

Colostrum is vital

The mare normally provides the foal with far more than comfort,
company and warm food. The foal's entire future depends on his
receiving colostrum in the first 12 hours of life.

Colostrum, the mare's "first milk," is a thick, creamy, yellow-white
substance that is extremely high in antibodies to virtually every disease (or vaccination) to which the mare has been exposed. **Unlike
most mammals, a mare does not transfer antibodies to her baby
while it is in the womb, which means that he is born without any
way to fight off bacteria and viruses.** The newborn foal's intestinal
tract can absorb antibodies intact from colostrum without digesting
them. Colostrum gives the foal's immune system a head start in fighting the many infections challenging him from the moment he leaves
the protected, sterile environment of the womb.

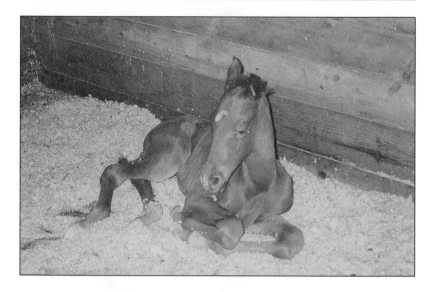

Your newborn foal requires colostrum within the first 12 hours of life in order to have antibodies to fight off an invasion of viruses and bacteria. If the mare can't supply colostrum, you must.

However, the ability to absorb the antibodies in colostrum declines very rapidly after he's about 12 hours old and is virtually gone 24 hours after birth. From that point onward, the intestinal tract will digest the antibodies, breaking down the proteins into much smaller pieces that can be used more easily by all the cells of the body. Separate from the foal's timetable, the mare produces colostrum for only about 48 hours, so milk from a mare who foaled a week ago won't do the job.

Life-threatening infections

If a foal is too weak to stand and nurse, or if the mare dies during or soon after delivery, there is a strong likelihood the foal will not receive the necessary amount of colostrum. Since it is virtually impossible to raise a foal in a sterile environment — and his immune system is still too immature to respond to vaccinations — even completely isolating the foal will not protect him from potentially harmful viruses, bacteria and fungi. The chance of his getting a life-threatening infection of some kind is very high.

In the case of mares who die during or recently after foaling, it may be possible to milk out the colostrum from the udder, assuming milk "let-down" — the process that allows the milk to be released from the mammary gland and flow freely through the teats — occurs before she dies. If milk let-down has been initiated, collect as much colostrum as you can from the udder of the mare. The container used to collect colostrum need not be sterile but must have been carefully cleaned with hot, soapy water and just as carefully rinsed. **A 110-pound foal will require a minimum of about 1.5 quarts of colostrum to provide him with sufficient antibody levels in his blood to ward off disease.**

In the event that you cannot milk out any, or enough, colostrum from the mare, an alternative source of colostrum will be needed. Many large breeding farms, veterinary schools and equine veterinarians have colostrum banks. You should call around to locate a source of frozen colostrum well in advance of the foaling date. Perhaps your veterinarian maintains a frozen supply for ready treatment of weak or orphaned foals. **Colostrum frozen and under proper storage temperature will remain "good" for approximately one year.** Colostrum must be kept frozen at -15° to -20° C. If it becomes thawed, even partially, and then refrozen, the sensitive protein in the antibodies will be destroyed.

Once colostrum has been obtained, you will often be racing the clock to get it into the foal in time. This is definitely a time when the veterinarian's assistance is best. **The most effective and easiest way to get colostrum where it needs to go is to administer it by stomach tube.** If you cannot get veterinary help in time but have the colostrum, put it in a livestock feeding bottle with a lamb-size nipple and encourage the foal to suckle.

When colostrum is obtained from horses who are not from your farm, it may be lacking in antibodies to dangerous bacteria specific to your premises. For this reason, it is often advisable to place foals orphaned at birth on a course of prophylactic (preventative) antibiotics. Your veterinarian can advise you regarding the types and dosages of antibiotics to use.

If you are unable to get colostrum into the foal in time (i.e., within 12 hours of birth), or if specific blood tests of the foal run by your veterinarian show that not enough has been absorbed, an additional source of antibodies will be needed. Products for administering preformed antibodies (gamma globulins) intravenously are commercially available. The protection they afford, however, is often not adequate. The best course, if at all possible, is to transfuse the horse with a serum preparation made from a live donor horse, preferably from your farm or one nearby, but this must be done under laboratory conditions.

Once the immediate problem of getting adequate colostrum or its equivalent has been solved, life settles down to a feeding routine. **Orphaned foals must be kept on either a foster mare (sometimes called a "nurse mare") or a commercial milk replacer for eight to 12 weeks for optimal nutrition and growth.**

Foster mares

Getting a mare to accept another mare's foal is no small feat. Some animals, such as cats, often share maternal duties, and a mother with babies will often accept another baby. But, horses bond very closely and specifically to their own foals. They usually reject the advances of other foals — and none too gently, either!

However, there are a small number of mares who will accept a strange foal. These will mother orphans either along with their own foals or after their foals have been weaned. (To find a nurse mare, you should contact the same sources we recommended for colostrum.)

There are techniques suggested for "forcing" reluctant mares to accept a foal — such as tranquilizing and physically restraining the mare or keeping the mare and foal separated by a barrier when the mare is not restrained for nursing. However, such tactics are far from 100 percent successful and will usually result in a relationship between the foal and the mare that is less than satisfactory (i.e., the mare may stop short of actually injuring the foal, but she will not bond).

It is the exceptional mare who will allow another mare's foal to nurse. Mares bond very specifically with their own foals.

Hand-raising foals

Although foals have been raised on the milk of other animals both with and without supplementation, there are major differences between mare's milk and that of other animals. Mare's milk contains 11.6% solids (i.e., constituents other than water). Cow and goat milks are similar, at 12.3% and 13.2% respectively, but the milks of ewes and sows are far more concentrated, at 19.3% and 20.1%.

In preparing milk replacer, measure powder into a graduated container and add water to bring up to the desired volume. Photo shows feeding bottle, lamb-size nipple and Foal-Lac.

The fat content of mare's milk is 15%, but the milk of cows, goats, ewes and sows has at least twice as much. Further analysis of the solids (or dry matter) of mare's milk shows 22.8% protein and a high level of sugars at 59.5%. The other species mentioned produce milk with slightly more protein (25% to 32%) and with far less sugar (24% to 38%). The point is, as with human babies, your best bet for feeding orphaned foals is to "use a formula designed specifically for them."

Foal-Lac, manufactured by Pet-Ag Inc., is an industry leader in equine milk replacers. A powdered formula for young foals and a pellet for older foals can be used, along with creep feed. The chart on page 199 in our appendix provides a recommended schedule for feeding milk replacer to foals between the ages of one day and two weeks. Many digestive problems stem from feeding too much at a time and not enough feedings throughout the day. Even the rigorous recommended schedule results in feeding far less frequent than natural feeding habits.

Digestive upsets, including bloating and diarrhea, are fairly common in hand-raised foals. Although these problems are more likely to occur when using either cow's or goat's milk, they may also arise when using milk replacers formulated for horses. (Occasionally foals don't adapt well to milk-replacer formulas but will grow well on cow's or goat's milk. However, you should first try the correct formula.)

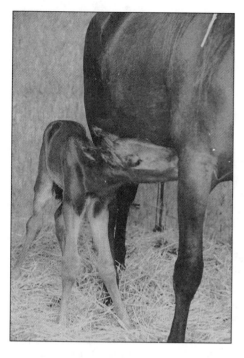

Newborn foals don't know exactly where to suckle.

A one-week-old foal will nurse an average of seven times an hour. Even at 24 weeks old, he's still nursing three times an hour. This avoids overloading the relatively small capacity of the foal's stomach and digestive tract. When using milk replacers, it is possible to feed less frequently, since they contain a higher percentage of solids (are more concentrated) than natural mare's milk. Formulated this way for the caretaker's convenience, however, they may not agree with the foal.

If digestive problems arise, they are best approached by dividing the recommended quantity of feed over more feedings. Milk replacer should not be used diluted unless directly ordered by the veterinarian. Failure to feed full-strength milk replacer deprives the foal of needed energy and will rapidly result in electrolyte imbalances that could lead to weakness or even death. If diluted milk must be fed (as in the case of a foal with severe, unresponsive diarrhea), the veterinarian will usually supplement calories and electrolytes in the form of an intravenous feeding or oral mixture.

You can assist the foal in digesting milk replacer by feeding yogurt containing live cultures (about one cup, divided among a day's feedings). Probiotic products containing live organisms can also be used (see Chapter 17 about iron toxicity, however), but the benefit would be about the same, especially when the foal is on the milk-replacer-only diet.

Another product we recommend is Ration Plus (Ration Plus for Horses), a dark brown fluid. It contains no live bacteria but is obtained by a special process from cultures of rapidly dividing beneficial bacteria. This product encourages the growth of all species of normal and helpful bacteria. It is well accepted and economical.

When feeding milk replacer, very young foals should be fed from a livestock bottle with a lamb-size nipple. The formula should be prepared fresh and fed comfortably warm. The old "shake a few drops onto your wrist" technique for testing the temperature of formula works just fine.

Older, stronger foals can be taught to drink from a bucket. Capitalizing on the foal's very strong instinct to nurse/suckle, dip your fingers in the formula, allowing the foal to suck your fingers while slowly bringing his muzzle closer and closer to the formula in the bucket each time you dip in. If you are successful in getting the foal to drink from a bucket, you will save yourself a lot of time.

Many digestive and diarrhea problems can be avoided by meticulous attention to cleanliness. While a mare's udder isn't always perfectly clean, the milk inside is. Feeding equipment and utensils used in preparation should be thoroughly cleansed with hot, soapy water and rinsed well after each feeding and stored appropriately.

Time to wean

Once the orphan foal is eight to 12 weeks old, weaning from milk can begin. Allow him access to small amounts of grass or high-quality hay (his interest in hay or grass will probably not be especially high just yet). You should select a grain ration specially formulated for growing horses and follow manufacturer's recommendations rigidly.

While many horses may do well on plain oats, some do not, and the result is stunted growth or less than optimal joint cartilage or bone. Once formed, it is too late. Even foals who appear to be doing well may have weaknesses, such as osteochondrosis or other bone/joint/tendon problems that will not become obvious until much later in life.

Eating manure

The foal will need to have a good start on developing a population of microorganisms in his intestinal tract that are capable of assisting in digestion. **Under normal circumstances, foals can regularly be seen eating their mother's manure.** While not appealing, it is a mechanism for getting the correct bacteria and other organisms into the foal's digestive system.

Unless the orphan is turned out in an area regularly used by other horses, he will not have access to this source of organisms. You should place a small amount of fresh manure in the foal's stall on a daily basis. In addition, the many probiotic products on the market are intended to help this process. These can be of benefit. However, yogurt and probiotics contain limited numbers of organisms and in far less variety than is present in normal manure. A combination of access to normal manure and use of Ration Plus, which will help greatly in getting the organisms established, is an inexpensive and effective way to manage this problem.

No doubt your mind jumps immediately to the one drawback of exposure to manure — the possibility of parasites. The last thing an orphan foal needs is the burden of a parasite load.

You can deworm your foal at four weeks using a piperazine product. (Consult with your veterinarian about the advisability of deworming any earlier.) After this, we would recommend the use of ivermectin every three to four weeks. Later, when the foal is eating his grain ration eagerly and predictably, you may want to switch to a Strongid C (Pfizer) daily worming program.

Housing and exercise

Initially, keep your foal confined in a dry, well-ventilated, well-bedded, safe stall or enclosed, sheltered area. A careful check should be made for projections, jagged edges and other hazards he could injure himself on. He requires a little more room for his size than an older horse — space to play and check out his legs. A large foaling stall is perfect.

But, even a roomy stall is not adequate space for a foal to exercise. Nature intends the foal be ready to travel with the herd within hours of birth, and, no doubt, your foal will be anxious to move around and try out his legs. The correct development and strengthening of muscles, tendons, ligaments and joints requires exercise.

Once the foal is steady on his feet, as early as a few days of age, you can begin leading him around outside and introducing him to the world. Do not just turn him out in a paddock and leave him. If he becomes frightened and has no one to turn to, he could easily panic and injure himself.

Pick a small paddock that allows the foal to run a little bit without having to pull up short every few strides to avoid slamming into things. Take 15- to 20-minute walks three times a day. Introduce him to the paddock on these walks. Once he seems familiar with it, you can turn him loose. Close observation and short periods of turnout should be the rule for the first week or so.

Tight, well-maintained wire mesh or chain link is ideal fencing for babies. Smooth pipe fencing is also safer than the more conventional board or post and rail arrangements that may tempt the foal to try to squeeze through — maybe even to follow you!

Do not turn your orphan foal into a pasture with other animals, even horses, as he'll likely try to nurse on nearly anything that moves and get himself injured.

Companionship and socialization

Horses are highly social animals. They bond first and most importantly with their dams. As they mature, they learn to play by interacting with other foals. The desire to be with other animals is very strong, and isolation will make a foal anxious. (Any orphan being fed on the recommended schedule will not remain alone too long, of course; nor will you.)

However, he needs more than human companionship if he is to grow up and take his place in the world of horses. Small companion animals, such as goats (does only, please!) or sheep, go a long way toward calming a foal and providing him with diversion and someone to play with. Still, it is important for the foal to learn how to be a horse. Young foals will benefit from having a calm, old pony for a companion, one who will tolerate the high energy and ceaseless efforts to be nursed by the foal. At least part of the foal's day (i.e., turnout times) should be spent with the pony as role model, hopefully with other horses close enough to be seen and smelled.

The foal should also have proximity to other horses — through stall bars or across wire partitions or by hanging out in the aisles to talk with the neighbors. If there are other foals on the farm, the orphan should be able to see them at play with each other and with their dams, and ideally he should be able to communicate with them across a fence line. As weaning time approaches, this contact will pay off when the weanlings can be turned out one or two at a time with their more independent orphan stablemate.

Safety must be the cardinal rule when introducing the orphan. However, proper socialization is a critical element in raising an orphan foal and should not be ignored.

If you do not have any other horses, perhaps you should begin by borrowing or purchasing an old pony to be your orphan's companion. Then, as the foal gets older, ask around or advertise for other

Socialization is important. Orphaned foals, especially, need playmates of their own kind.

weanlings to be companions. Any number of people in your area might be glad to find a way to separate their mare and foal at weaning time, reducing their own weanling's trauma with a companion.

Then again, you might board your weaning-age orphan on a farm that has other weanlings, at least for a few months.

Mom's fine, but no milk

There are other problems that can result in insufficient colostrum intake. On the mare's side, she may not let down her milk soon enough or in sufficient amount for the foal to get the required amount of colostrum. Even if the mare's milk becomes available in time, she may not produce enough milk, or her milk may not contain a good concentration of antibodies.

First-time mothers are also often nervous about letting the foal nurse, either because of inexperience or discomfort. **Gentle, patient restraint of the mare, with one person reassuring her while another guides the foal in the right direction, will usually work.** ▣

For contact information on specific products mentioned, please see page 204.

22

Metabolic Bone Disease

What you can do to prevent serious —
potentially crippling — growth disorders.

Everyone breeding horses wants a foal who is "correct" and stands straight. Selecting a sire and broodmare with good conformation is important in producing athletic, well-conformed foals. We go to great lengths to breed for size, disposition, athletic ability and correct conformation. One of the least known factors in growing "correct" babies, however, is metabolic bone disease, which can wreak havoc in their growth and development.

Metabolic bone disease may be defined as a disorder of the growth or formation of bone and associated joint structures. A broad category, metabolic bone disease includes such problems as:

■ Osteochondrosis dessicans (OCD)
■ Epiphysitis
■ Contracted tendons
■ Angular limb deformities
■ Incomplete ossification of bones
■ Wobbler's syndrome
■ Bran disease ("big head").

Most breeders hear these terms, though few know what they actually mean. We'll give you a thumbnail version of each problem later in this chapter, but the important news is that you can play a significant role in preventing these problems.

The causes of metabolic bone disease are varied, including hereditary factors, prenatal conditions, trauma, hormonal fluctuations, and nutritional imbalances.

Prevention of metabolic bone disease begins long before the foal is born; proper nutrition for pregnant mares is crucial.

Nutritional imbalances

Nutrition is a major factor in the development of all types of metabolic bone disease. With the exception of cases where an extremely abnormal diet is being fed, such as with bran disease (in which you also see symptoms in the mare), **an apparently normal mare can give birth to a foal having metabolic bone disease from nutritional causes**. This means that if you are feeding a pregnant mare, taking the time to learn about proper nutrition may make the difference between a great baby and a crooked-legged one.

As you might imagine, calcium plays a major role in the development of strong bones. **Insufficient amounts of calcium, or calcium in improper ratio to phosphorus, may result in metabolic bone disease.** Less known is that calcium excesses are not as dangerous as phosphorus excesses, providing that the total amount of phosphorus being consumed is adequate for the size and age of the horse.

Simply put, once a horse receives an adequate level of phosphorus, beyond that point he can deal better with extra calcium than extra phosphorus, but the right balance should be attempted, especially for proper bone growth in young horses. Because alfalfa is typically high in calcium, you should be careful to include adequate amounts of feed containing phosphorus in an alfalfa-based diet. On the other hand, if you are depending on a grass hay and grain diet for your broodmare, you are more likely to have too much phosphorus than too much calcium.

The most graphic example of a purely nutritionally generated metabolic bone disease is "bran disease." This disorder is found in horses fed high amounts of grain or bran but little forage, or in the foals of mares fed a phosphorus-excessive diet.

In a famous retrospective study of metabolic bone disease in foals, the rations on various farms were analyzed and compared with the incidence of metabolic bone disease. The lowest number of cases were on farms that fed 1.2% calcium in the diet, the highest from those that fed only 0.2% calcium.

WHEN EVALUATING A FEED, REMEMBER THAT THE NUMBERS YOU ARE STRIVING TO ACHIEVE MUST APPLY TO THE ENTIRE RATION — HAY AND GRAIN.

Studies have also shown that the minerals copper and zinc also play critical roles in the development of strong and straight bones. Copper levels of 40 to 60 ppm (mg/kg of dry matter of diet) are felt to be needed, with zinc as high as 90 ppm for pregnant mares. These numbers are far in excess of the current NRC estimates of required levels. However, very little true research has been done on these minerals in horses. The NRC's numbers are really based on what the average horse usually eats without showing signs of a full-blown, possibly life-threatening deficiency. **There is a wide chasm between the level of a nutrient necessary to sustain life and that which is optimal for pregnancy, lactation, growth, development and athletic performance.**

The mare also requires sufficient energy (calories) to maintain pregnancy, lactation and growth without becoming thin. This may sound too nonspecific and vague, but it describes the situation more accurately than if we were to quote guidelines for ratios of pounds of grain/hay to feed. Feeding charts are useful as a starting point but cannot take into consideration the individual variations in requirements, changes necessitated by feed quality, or changes in the mare's circumstances. In short, good horsemanship will tell you to feed your mare enough to keep her looking good, not obese or thin.

What about protein?

Growing up, we all saw the ads advising us to drink milk — not just for the calcium but also for the protein. Protein is a critical consideration in animals, too, while forming bones and joints. **Growing animals require not only a larger amount of protein (14% or more for horses) than older animals, but also protein of a very high quality, easily digestible and containing the proper amounts of amino acids.** Milk is the perfect food for nursing foals, but the switch to feed can be a real problem. The protein in some diets is only about 50% digestible, meaning that the feed you thought was giving your foal 14% protein actually yields only 7%.

While there is no doubt that the amino acid composition is very important, we do not really know what is optimal for growing horses. **On the basis of controlled scientific studies, lysine is the only amino acid known to be essential for growth;** however, it is almost

Mares will produce a perfectly balanced milk at the expense of their own body, making good broodmare nutrition important for the health of both mare and foal.

universally agreed that attention must be paid to the sulfur-containing amino acids such as methionine. Others are probably "essential" in the diet, but as of now, we simply do not have that information.

For years we've cited excessive protein in the diet to be a cause of metabolic bone disease, but research has not confirmed this. Excessive calorie intake and the resultant abnormally rapid growth rate is now felt to be a more likely cause. Again, good barn management would have you look at your foals and weanlings to determine if they are getting too much energy (calories) or about the right amount.

Finally, vitamin D, the "sunshine vitamin," is critical to the formation of bones and joints. Horses exposed to an adequate amount of sun will not only manufacture sufficient amounts but will store it in their livers for times of need (such as long, dark winters). This is fine for the adult horse, but foals are born with extremely low levels of vitamin D, a consideration particularly if your foal is born very early in the year. Your veterinarian may decide it is wise to supplement a foal for a brief period of time, usually by injection. **EXCESS VITAMIN D IS EXTREMELY TOXIC and is capable of causing abnormalities**. For this reason, it is inadvisable for owners and farm managers to take it upon themselves to supplement foals with vitamin D without consulting their veterinarian.

Very little is known about vitamin C in the horse, but we do know that it has a major role in the proper formation of bones, joint cartilage and ligamentous tissue. Since, unlike man, horses manufacture their own vitamin C, they do not spontaneously develop levels low enough to cause scurvy – the classic deficiency disease. Still, lots of room is left for problems related to low vitamin C levels. Bone and joint abnormalities are also commonly seen in other species which can manufacture their own vitamin C, and the problems reverse when vitamin C is added to the diet. **Since it has been shown that stress can lower vitamin C blood levels in horses, supplementation may be advisable during times of stress, such as foaling, shipping, illness, weaning and so forth.**

Hereditary factors

Metabolic bone disease appears to run in families. It is not clear whether heredity is the primary factor in defects in bone or cartilage metabolics or a problem related to the proper absorption or utilization of nutrients. It pays to look at the history, particularly of the mare that you are breeding, as well as the foals she has produced.

Types of metabolic bone disease

Osteochondrosis dessicans results in abnormalities of the joint cartilage and subchondral (under the cartilage) bone. Lesions include thinning of the cartilage, formation of cartilage flaps, bone cysts under joint areas and joint "mice" (loose pieces of broken-off cartilage that float freely in the joint).

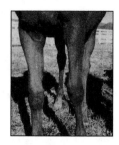

Epiphysitis is swelling/inflammation and enlargement of the "growth plate" regions of the bones. Most commonly involved areas include the knee and fetlock.

Angular limb deformities commonly affect the knees of growing horses.

Contracted tendons is a condition in which the forelegs become increasingly straight, with loss of angulation at the fetlock and a taut, stretched appearance to the flexor tendons.

Angular limb deformity is a growth abnormality in which one side of the bone appears to be growing faster than the other, leading the legs to "turn out," either from below the knee, below the ankle, or both.

Incomplete ossification is a condition where a horse is born with soft bone that has not been completely calcified. Most commonly involved are the small bones of the hock or knee. On X-ray, these bones are either "invisible" or very faint.

Wobbler's syndrome is a deformity of the articulations of the cervical spine (neck).

Bran disease ("big head") is a condition whose most dramatic feature is enlargement of the bones of the upper and lower jaw, and facial crest. Less dramatic cases, as well as the advanced ones, also show abnormalities of the articular cartilage and subchondral bone, as are found in osteochondrosis dessicans.

Prenatal conditions

Prenatal (before birth) conditions may contribute to problems such as angular limb deformities. Large foals are sometimes quite cramped within the uterus, causing the limbs to be "crooked" at birth. If there is no underlying bone or joint disease, these foals will often straighten out on their own or can be corrected by a short period of casting. Extreme cases may require surgery. However, in all cases of angular limb deformities, metabolic bone disease must be considered. Incomplete ossification may occur simply because a foal is born prematurely, with no bone or joint disease being responsible.

Hormonal fluctuations

Normal growth and development of bones and joints is strongly influenced by such hormones as growth hormone, parathyroid hormone and thyroid hormone. **It is less likely that metabolic bone disease will result from a hormone problem than from a nutritional imbalance, but the possibility exists and must be considered in cases where a nutritional imbalance is not obvious.**

The safest and easiest approach to correct nutrition for weanlings is to use a complete commercial feed designed to prevent metabolic bone disease.

Trauma

Some cases of metabolic bone disease may have a traumatic origin, particularly late-developing angular limb deformities, epiphysitis or OCD involving a single joint. Trauma to cartilage or bone, or crushing of these delicate tissues by excessive body weight or weight distributed in an unusual manner, can easily disrupt the blood supply and result in metabolic bone disease.

What can you do?

Aside from the obvious good choice of sire and dam, the best way to attack metabolic bone disease is by providing optimal nutrition, beginning with the mare early in her pregnancy. We've mentioned important factors: energy, protein, calcium and phosphorus, and copper and zinc. But how do you assure that your mare is getting what she needs?

One approach is to consult an equine nutritionist (through a veterinary school or feed company or your local agricultural extension agency). You will need to be armed with a complete breakdown of the nutritional composition of your hay and grain. The nutritionist can analyze the data and suggest a supplement program, which will more than likely consist primarily of a mineral mix. If your ration is top quality, both hay and grains, the mix may be the way to proceed, assuming you can get the mare and foal to actually consume the required amounts of minerals on a regular, daily basis. (Most horses will not do this on their own.) Another problem with attempting to supplement inadequate rations is that the nutritional composition of the hay you are using will most likely change over time, even over a few months.

Supplementing the diet of mares with mineral mix may be appropriate, but foals often will not consume the required amount on a regular basis.

Another approach, which makes more sense for most people, is to take advantage of the expertise of a major

Adequate exercise and a safe environment is important to normal development of bones and joints.

equine feed manufacturer and use a feed designed to prevent metabolic bone disease problems. Several large feed companies have upgraded their rations for mares and foals to provide the higher levels of copper and zinc that appear to be needed for optimal bone and joint formation.

When evaluating a feed, remember that the numbers you are striving to achieve must apply to the entire ration – hay and grain. If you buy a grain that supplies the recommended 50 ppm of copper and 90 ppm of zinc, but only feed two or three pounds a day along with free-choice hay (which will be double or triple that amount), your numbers will not yield the same parts per million that you intended. In other words, a properly balanced grain fed with three times as much hay is not necessarily balanced anymore. You may have paid for an expensive concentrate that doesn't work with what else you're feeding.

A compromise might be to supplement the mares (who are more likely to tolerate a mineral mix added to their grain) and go with a complete balanced feed for your growing horses.

Coupled with common sense measures — like minimizing injury with a safe environment, routine health maintenance (worming and vaccination) and meticulous attention to proper trimming and foot care — a preventative nutritional approach is your main weapon in the fight against metabolic bone disease.

Easy nutrition for young horses

Equine Junior (Purina) is a leader in nutrition for foals and older growing horses. It is designed to be fed from weaning to the age of two and provides all the nutrients needed for optimal growth, including bone and joints. The patented fat and protein pellet is highly digestible, energy dense and extremely stable in storage, and amounts of feed are easy to adjust during periods of rapid growth. Because it is a complete feed, hay is not necessary, and in fact, there is a limit to the amount of hay you can feed without interfering with the overall nutrient balance of the diet. This concept may make some people uncomfortable, but it is not harmful to the horse. Those who feel they must feed hay, or some other roughage, can contact the manufacturer directly for guidelines. ◧⊞

Appendix

Normal Physiological Data for Adult Horses

Temperature: 99° to 101° F
Pulse: High 20s to low 40s beats per minute
Respiration: 8 to 20 breaths per minute
Mucous membrane color: Pale pink to medium pink
Capillary refill time: 1 to 3 seconds

Note: All figures will be higher for foals. Weather conditions and time of day will cause variances in these numbers.

Sample Feeding Schedule for Foal Weighing 110 lbs. at Birth

Age in days	1	2	3-5	6-8	9-11	12-14	15 up
Daily feedings	16	14	12	10	8	7	5
Time between feedings (hours)							
Day	1.5	1.5	2	2	3	3	4
Night	1.5	2.0	2	3	3	4	6
Grams of powder per feeding	30	45	75	120	180	250	310
Volume of prepared replacer per feeding (liters)	0.25	0.40	0.6	1.0	1.5	2.0	2.5

Adapted from Feeding the Sick or Orhaned Foal, *Currect Therapy in Equine Medicine*, 2 N.E. Robinson (ed), 1987

Conversion Factors

Metric Equivalents
LINEAR MEASURE
1 centimeter ....0.3937 inch
1 inch ....2.54 centimeters
1 meter ....1.0936 yds.
1 yard ....0.9144 meter
1 kilometer ....0.62137 mile
1 mile ....1.6094 kilometers

SQUARE MEASURE
1 sq. centimeter ....0.1550 sq. inch
1 sq. inch ....6.452 sq. centimeters
1 sq. meter..................1.196 sq. yards
1 sq. yard ....0.8361 sq. meter

MEASURE OF VOLUME
1 cu. centimeter ....0.061 cu. inch
1 cu. inch ....16.39 cu. centimeters
1 cu. yard ....0.7646 cu. meter
1 liter ....1.0567 qts. liq.
1 quart dry.......................1.101 liters
1 quart liquid ....0.9463 liter

WEIGHTS
1 gram ....0.03527 ounce
1 ounce ....28.35 grams
1 kilogram ....2.2046 pounds
1 pound ....0.4536 kilogram
1 metric ton ......0.98421 English ton
1 English ton ....1.016 metric ton

GRAIN CONVERSION
1 quart of oats ....1lb.
1 quart of corn ....approx 2 lb.
1 quart of sweet feed ..approx 1.5 lb.
1 quart dry bran ....0.5 lb.

U.S. Measures
LIQUID MEASURE
30 ml......................................1 ounce
8 ounces ....1 cup
2 cups...1 pint
2 pints ....1 quart
4 quarts...................................1 gallon

LONG MEASURE
12 inches ....1 foot
3 feet ....1 yard
5½ yards ....1 rod
40 rods ....1 furlong
8 furlongs ....1 statute mile
5,280 feet.................................1 mile
3 nautical miles ....1 league

CUBIC MEASURE
1,728 cu. in ....1 cu. ft.
27 cu. ft ....1 cu. yd.
128 cu. ft......................1 cord (wood)
40 cu. ft ....1 ton (shipping)

DRY MEASURE
2 pints ....1 quart
8 quarts ....1 peck
4 pecks..................................1 bushel

TEMPERATURES
To convert degrees F to degrees C ....
   subtract 32, then multiply by 5/9
To convert degrees C to degrees F ....
   multiply by 9/5, then add 32
0° C ....32° F

APPROXIMATE HOUSEHOLD MEASURES
1 teaspoon ....5 ml
3 teaspoons...................1 tablespoon

OTHER HELPFUL NOTES
4 inch ....1 head
1 ml ....1 cc
1,000 milligrams ....1 gram
1,000 grams ....1 kilogram
ppm (parts per million) ....mg/kg